even better BROWNIES

50 Standout Bar Recipes for Every Occasion

MIKE JOHNSON

Creator of Mike Bakes NYC

Copyright © 2020 Michael Johnson

First published in 2020 by
Page Street Publishing Co.
27 Congress Street, Suite 105
Salem, MA 01970
www.pagestreetpublishing.com

All rights reserved. No part of this book may be reproduced or used, in any form or by any means, electronic or mechanical, without prior permission in writing from the publisher.

Distributed by Macmillan, sales in Canada by The Canadian Manda Group.

24   23   22   4 5

ISBN-13: 978-1-64567-092-6
ISBN-10: 1-64567-092-9

Library of Congress Control Number: 2019957327

Cover and book design by Rosie Stewart for Page Street Publishing Co.
Photography by Michael Johnson

Printed and bound in China

Page Street Publishing protects our planet by donating to nonprofits like The Trustees, which focuses on local land conservation.

contents

Introduction

Growing up, baking from scratch wasn't a massive part of my daily life. I learned the basics by making cookies from a recipe on the chocolate chips bag. And I have fond memories of my grandma's kitchen, stirring oil and eggs into boxed cake mixes. Moving into my first college apartment, I brought with me a reliable brownie recipe, the belief that the only frosting worth using came in a can with tiny rainbow chips in the lid and the certainty that baking anything more complicated than box mixes required magical powers I simply didn't possess.

But college has a way of eroding certainties, and so I eventually challenged myself to try baking new things. I learned that, sure, there is some magic to baking a toe-curlingly good cookie (as it turns out, that magic is mostly science), but there is also patience and care and not mixing up the baking soda and baking powder or sugar and salt. It was something I could do and something I grew to love. So, I did it a lot.

My twenties, so far, have been a story written mainly in sugar and chocolate. I've taught myself the science behind baking, I've tried new techniques, and I've developed new and exciting recipes. Writing for my blog has taught not only me but also my readers a ton of useful lessons about baking. For instance, I've learned that more isn't always better. No matter how much you love an ingredient, or how pretty it is, if you go overboard with it, you'll ruin your recipe. And sometimes, a flavor that works great as a stand-alone just doesn't translate well into a cookie or brownie. (Looking at you, cotton candy.)

As with any learning experience, especially in the baking world, there have been successes and failures—and by failures, I mean utter disasters. Becoming a baking blogger has given me the opportunity and luxury to experiment and step out of my comfort zone with more involved and technical recipes. However, as a busy millennial working a traditional 9 to 5 while also putting in full-time hours on my blog, I still crave those simple, never-fail recipes that can be turned out with the essential staple pantry items I always have on hand. This was the driving inspiration behind most of the recipes in this book.

In this book, you'll find 50 recipes for homemade brownies and bars. This cookbook is designed to satisfy both skilled bakers and beginner bakers alike. There are essential dessert recipes that every home cook should know, as well as innovative, insanely fresh recipes that I hope you're excited to try. The ingredients are *mostly* everyday items that are affordable and easy to find in your local supermarket or on Amazon—and may already be in your pantry. And I've kept prep times short because I know firsthand how busy life can be.

I know this book will help you create some of your favorite desserts, and I hope it'll also help you discover some new favorites. But even more than that, I hope these recipes will show you what treasures can be made with simple ingredients and that they inspire you to get in the kitchen and have fun baking them yourself!

Mike Johnson

out of this world brownies

They say laughter's the best medicine. But they lied. It's brownies. I mean honestly . . . brownies can make just about any situation ten times better. Going through a breakup? Brownies. Stuck entertaining a crowd? Brownies. Mandatory work potluck? Bring brownies. (I think you get the picture.)

When it comes to desserts, I tend to gravitate more toward vanilla and fruity things rather than chocolate. I mean, I like chocolate in things, but I generally don't like strictly chocolate-flavored things. Does that make any sense at all? One exception to that, however, is brownies; I'm pretty smitten with brownies and probably always will be. Served piping hot or at room temperature, made from scratch or from a box mix, brownies are quite possibly one of the most versatile desserts out there. They're easy to make, even easier to eat and there are about a million delicious variations.

Brownies can be fudgy almost to the point of completely under-baked gooeyness, or they can masquerade as chocolate cake. They can be bitter enough to provoke a twinge behind the ears or so sweet you wonder where the chocolate went. Then there's the whole nuts/no nuts controversy. And, of course, the fans of a pretty, shiny top vs. a crackly meringue-like top. Then there are those who say, "Who cares, so long as it's chocolate?" In short, to each his own. Whether you enjoy the dense texture of a basic fudgy brownie or the fluffy goodness of cake-like versions, brownies do the trick when you want a fast-to-make snack or dessert that's oh-so-delicious.

The brownies in this chapter are genuinely some of my favorite recipes that I've ever developed. There are the Ultimate Fudge Brownies (page 13), which are the Old Faithful of my brownie collection, the recipe I always give to new bakers, knowing they'll love it and that they'll always be successful with it. And the Bourbon-Pecan Brownies (page 30), the recipe I turn to when I want a boozy-yet-sweet pick-me-up. And don't even get me started on the showstopping, life-changing S'mores Brownies (page 25); I'm not being dramatic—they're really that good.

Let's get chocolate-wasted, shall we?

TIPS & TECHNIQUES

- Use high-quality chocolate bars or chocolate chips. Brownies don't require a lot of ingredients, so the ones you use should be really great. Instead of merely purchasing "baking chocolate," grab chocolate bars that you'd want to eat on their own.

- Also, when it comes to chocolate chips, standard chocolate chips often contain stabilizers and preservatives to help them keep their shape, which makes their melting process and flavor profile different from baking chocolate. To avoid any mishaps in your recipe, opt for high-quality baking bars or feves.

- Check on your brownies before the recommended time. Brownies (like most baked goods) are sensitive creatures. A few minutes too long in the oven, and you'll wave bye-bye to their ideal texture. For best results, follow the baking time in the recipe and check them 5 minutes before the timer buzzes since every oven (and baking pan) is different. If you do overbake them, don't worry. Slather the top with chocolate frosting or ganache before cutting, or, if they're beyond eating altogether, crumble them into an ice cream sundae.

- Let the brownies cool completely. I know how delicious warm brownies can be, so it can be tempting to slice into them right away. Cutting brownies too soon after baking, however, is a messy business. The brownies will continue to set as they cool down, as well as develop flavor. Plus, they slice and come out of the pan much easier when adequately cooled. But, if the presentation doesn't matter and your appetite can't wait, then go for it!

TOTAL TIME: 1 hour 30 minutes
YIELD: 16 bars

ultimate fudge brownies

So often, ultimate fudge brownie recipes are disappointing (at least all the ones I've tried), but I'm here to change your views on that. Those "fudge" brownies that are drier than the Sahara Desert in the summertime? Never again. Brownies that are too sweet OR not sweet enough? No thanks. And brownies that are described as "chewy" but taste like chocolate cake? Later, dude. It's time to say goodbye to mediocre brownies and HELLO to the most amazing, ultimate fudge brownies ever.

4 oz (115 g) 70% cacao dark chocolate, chopped

2 tsp (4 g) espresso powder

6 tbsp (30 g) unsweetened natural or Dutch-process cocoa powder, divided

1 cup (230 g) unsalted butter

¾ cup (150 g) granulated sugar

½ cup (110 g) dark brown sugar

2 tsp (10 ml) vanilla extract

1 tsp kosher salt

3 large eggs

½ cup (60 g) all-purpose flour

Flaky sea salt, for topping, optional

Preheat the oven to 350°F (180°C). Grease an 8 x 8–inch (20 x 20–cm) pan with butter or nonstick cooking spray and then line the pan with parchment paper, leaving an overhang on all sides. Grease the parchment with butter or nonstick cooking spray and then set it aside.

In a medium, heatproof bowl, combine the chopped chocolate, espresso powder and 2 tablespoons (10 g) of cocoa powder and set aside.

Add the butter to a small saucepan over medium heat and cook until the butter just comes to a vigorous simmer, about 5 minutes, stirring often. Immediately pour the hot butter over the chocolate mixture and let it sit for 2 minutes. Whisk until the chocolate is completely smooth and melted, then set it aside.

In the bowl of a stand mixer fitted with the whisk attachment, or using an electric hand mixer, whisk together the granulated sugar, dark brown sugar, vanilla, salt and eggs for precisely 10 minutes.

With the mixer on, pour in the slightly cooled chocolate mixture and mix until smooth, about 2 minutes.

Sift in the flour and the remaining 4 tablespoons (20 g) of cocoa powder and use a rubber spatula to gently fold until just combined.

Pour the batter into the prepared pan and smooth the top with a spatula. Bake for 20 minutes, and then remove the pan from the oven and slam it on a flat surface two to three times (this deflates the brownies slightly, giving them a more even texture and encourages that beautiful crackly top). Return the pan to the oven and bake until a toothpick inserted into the center of the brownies comes out fudgy, but the edges look cooked through, about 10 additional minutes. The center of the brownies will seem under-baked, but the brownies will continue to cook and set as they cool.

Allow the brownies to cool completely in the pan. Use the parchment paper to lift the cooled brownies out of the pan. Sprinkle the top of the brownies with the flaky sea salt, if desired, and cut into 16 bars.

Cover and store leftover brownies in an airtight container at room temperature for 3 to 4 days.

TOTAL TIME: 1 hour 30 minutes
YIELD: 16 brownies

spiced caramel turtle brownies

If you are not familiar with "turtles," they're chocolate-covered caramel and pecan clusters, and let me just tell you that they're seriously addictive. The words "decadent" and "delicious" are how I would describe these fudgy brownies. When I was developing the recipe for these brownies, I wanted to pay homage to the OG chocolate turtles but also update the flavor in some way, which is why I decided to make a spiced caramel. The spices add subtle warmth and depth of flavor and really put these brownies over the top.

SPICED CARAMEL TOPPING

¼ cup (60 ml) heavy cream

¾ tsp kosher salt

¼ tsp ground cinnamon

⅛ tsp ground ginger

⅛ tsp ground cardamom

Pinch of cloves

Pinch of nutmeg

½ cup (100 g) granulated sugar

3 tbsp (43 g) unsalted butter

BROWNIES

6 tbsp (85 g) unsalted butter

3 oz (85 g) 70% cacao dark chocolate, chopped

½ cup (100 g) granulated sugar

½ cup (110 g) light brown sugar

2 large eggs

1 tsp vanilla extract

½ cup (45 g) unsweetened natural or Dutch-process cocoa powder

½ cup (60 g) all-purpose flour

½ tsp kosher salt

¾ cup (85 g) chopped pecans

Pecan halves, for topping, optional

Preheat the oven to 350°F (180°C). Grease an 8 x 8–inch (20 x 20–cm) pan with butter or nonstick cooking spray and then line the pan with parchment paper, leaving an overhang on all sides. Grease the parchment with butter or nonstick cooking spray and then set it aside.

To make the spiced caramel topping, in a small saucepan, heat the heavy cream, salt, cinnamon, ginger, cardamom, cloves and nutmeg over medium-low heat until the cream is scalded and lightly bubbling, about 5 minutes. Be careful not to let it boil! Remove the pan from the heat, cover it and set it aside until needed.

In a medium saucepan over medium heat, heat the granulated sugar, continually stirring with a high heat–resistant rubber spatula or wooden spoon. The sugar will form clumps and eventually melt into a thick, amber-colored liquid as you continue to stir. Be careful not to let it burn!

Once the sugar is completely melted, about 10 minutes, immediately add the butter and stir until the butter is melted, about 2 minutes. (Be careful with this step, because the caramel will bubble rapidly when the butter is added.) Very slowly drizzle in the spiced heavy cream while stirring. Allow the mixture to boil for 30 to 45 seconds and then remove from the heat. Allow the mixture to cool down at room temperature before using it.

To make the brownies, place the butter and chopped chocolate in a heatproof bowl and set the bowl over a pan of gently simmering water to create a double boiler. Stir occasionally until the chocolate is fully melted, 5 to 7 minutes. Remove the bowl from the heat and whisk in the granulated sugar and light brown sugar until thoroughly combined. Whisk in the eggs and vanilla, and then fold in the cocoa powder, flour and salt using a rubber spatula or wooden spoon. Fold in the chopped pecans until they are evenly incorporated. Be careful not to overmix!

(continued)

spiced caramel turtle brownies (continued)

Pour the batter into the prepared pan and bake for 25 minutes, and then test the brownies with a toothpick inserted into the center of the pan. If it comes out with wet batter, the brownies are not done. If there are only a few moist crumbs, the brownies are done. Keep checking the brownies every 2 minutes until you have moist crumbs.

Remove the pan from the oven and pour the slightly cooled spiced caramel topping on top of the hot brownies. Spread it evenly on top and then top with pecan halves, if using. Place the pan on a wire rack to cool completely before cutting into squares.

Cover and store leftover brownies in an airtight container at room temperature for 3 to 4 days.

TOTAL TIME: 1 hour 30 minutes
YIELD: 16 brownies

samoas brownies

Thin Mints may be the most popular Girl Scout cookies, but Samoas (or Caramel deLites, depending on your region) are definitely better. I mean, they have everything: a caramel coating, coconut and chocolate! Literally, what more could you want? Enter: Samoas Brownies. Imagine a fudgy-meets-cakey brownie base topped with coconut caramel and a final chocolate drizzle. Step aside, shortbread cookies, it's time for these brownies to carry the coconut-caramel torch of dessert glory!

BROWNIES

½ cup (115 g) unsalted butter

1 cup (175 g) semisweet chocolate chips, divided

¾ cup (150 g) granulated sugar

½ tbsp (8 ml) vanilla extract

1 tsp espresso powder

2 large eggs

¼ cup (30 g) all-purpose flour

¼ cup (20 g) unsweetened natural or Dutch-process cocoa powder

½ tsp baking powder

COCONUT-CARAMEL TOPPING

½ cup (100 g) granulated sugar

3 tbsp (43 g) unsalted butter, cubed

¼ cup (60 ml) heavy cream

1¼ cups (105 g) unsweetened shredded coconut flakes

2 oz (60 g) 70% cacao dark chocolate, melted

Preheat the oven to 350°F (180°C). Grease an 8 x 8–inch (20 x 20–cm) pan with butter or nonstick cooking spray and then line the pan with parchment paper, leaving an overhang on all sides. Grease the parchment with butter or nonstick cooking spray and then set it aside.

To make the brownies, place the butter and ¾ cup (130 g) of chocolate chips in a heatproof bowl and set it over a pan of gently simmering water to create a double boiler. Stir occasionally until the chocolate is fully melted. Remove the bowl from the heat and whisk in the granulated sugar, vanilla and espresso powder.

In a small bowl, whisk the eggs for 1 minute until bubbly on top. Stir the eggs into the chocolate mix. Add the flour, cocoa powder, baking powder and remaining ¼ cup (45 g) of chocolate chips and stir until just combined. Evenly spread the mixture into the prepared pan. Bake for 28 to 30 minutes, or until the brownies are just set.

To make the coconut-caramel topping, heat the granulated sugar in a medium saucepan over medium heat, stirring with a high heat–resistant rubber spatula or wooden spoon. The sugar will form clumps and eventually melt into a thick, amber-colored liquid as you continue to stir, about 10 minutes. Be careful not to let it burn! Once the sugar is completely melted, immediately add the butter and stir until the butter is melted, about 2 minutes. (Be careful with this step because the caramel will bubble rapidly when the butter is added.) Very slowly drizzle in the heavy cream while stirring. Allow the mixture to boil for 30 to 45 seconds and then remove it from the heat. Stir in the coconut flakes and set aside until the brownies are completely cool.

(continued)

samoas brownies (continued)

Spread the coconut-caramel topping on top of the brownies once they're cool. Run a knife along the edges of the pan so the brownies don't stick to the pan.

Spoon the melted chocolate into a small ziplock bag, creating a makeshift pastry bag. Cut a small hole at the bottom corner of the bag. Drizzle the melted chocolate over the coconut-caramel topping. Set the brownies in the fridge to cool for about 30 minutes before cutting.

Cover and store leftover brownies in an airtight container at room temperature for 3 to 4 days.

peanut butter cornflake crunch brownies

These brownies are inspired by Tieghan from Half Baked Harvest. They're basically a hybrid of Special K bars and a fudge brownie. You know what's really great about these brownies, though? They are incredibly easy to make—no secret ingredient and no step that involves some obscure tool you probably don't have. Just a lot of chocolate. And butter. And eggs. And peanut butter. And a little bit of sugar.

BROWNIES

6 tbsp (85 g) unsalted butter, melted

⅓ cup (80 ml) canola oil

2 tbsp (10 g) unsweetened natural or Dutch-process cocoa powder

2 tbsp (10 g) black cocoa powder (see Note)

2 large eggs

½ cup (100 g) granulated sugar

1 tsp vanilla extract

¾ cup (90 g) all-purpose flour

¼ tsp kosher salt

CORNFLAKE CRUNCH

¼ cup (60 ml) dark corn syrup

½ cup (130 g) creamy peanut butter

1 tsp vanilla extract

2 cups (50 g) cornflakes

CHOCOLATE DRIZZLE

3 oz (85 g) 70% cacao dark chocolate, chopped

1 tbsp (15 g) butter

Preheat the oven to 350°F (180°C). Grease an 8 x 8–inch (20 x 20–cm) pan with butter or nonstick cooking spray and then line the pan with parchment paper, leaving an overhang on all sides. Grease the parchment with butter or nonstick cooking spray and then set it aside.

To make the brownies, in a medium bowl, mix the butter and canola oil, add the unsweetened and black cocoa powders and stir until well blended. In a large bowl, beat the eggs with a mixer. Add the sugar and vanilla and beat well. Add the chocolate mixture and beat to combine. Slowly add in the flour and salt. Spread half of the brownie mixture evenly in the pan; it will make a very thin layer.

To make the cornflake crunch, in a large saucepan, mix the corn syrup and peanut butter together. Heat almost to a boil, being careful not to let it burn. Stir to combine the ingredients. Turn off the heat and stir in the vanilla. Then mix in the cornflakes. Drop about three-fourths of the cornflake mixture evenly over the brownie batter, saving the remaining cornflake mixture for later.

Spread the remaining brownie batter over the top of the cornflakes. (This will be hard since the batter is so thick, and you likely will not be able to cover the whole cornflake layer, which is OK.) Bake for 20 to 25 minutes. Test the brownies with a toothpick inserted into the center of the pan. If it comes out with wet batter, the brownies are not done. If there are only a few moist crumbs, the brownies are done.

To make the chocolate drizzle, in a small bowl, microwave the chopped chocolate and butter in 30-second increments until the chocolate is melted and smooth, about 1 minute.

Top the baked brownies with clusters of the remaining cornflake crunch, gently pressing the clusters down. Drizzle with melted chocolate and then allow the brownies to cool completely or refrigerate for 1 hour before serving. Cover and store leftover brownies in an airtight container at room temperature for 3 to 4 days.

NOTE: *Black cocoa is an ultra-Dutch-processed cocoa powder. The result is a cocoa powder that's completely mellow, non-bitter and very black. (Think Oreo cookies.) You can replace the black cocoa with an equal amount of regular or Dutch-processed cocoa if that's all you have on hand.*

TOTAL TIME: 1 hour 15 minutes
YIELD: 24 bars

peppermint mocha brownies

Peppermint Mocha Brownies are your favorite holiday latte in dessert form—as in brownies loaded with a hint of coffee and peppermint flavors shining through each bite, all decked out with crushed bits of striped candy canes sprinkled on top. 'Cause when it's the holidays, nothing screams FESTIVE quite like something sweet and totally, unapologetically over the top.

1 tbsp (15 ml) boiling water

1½ tbsp (9 g) espresso powder

1 cup (85 g) unsweetened natural or Dutch-process cocoa powder

1 cup (220 g) dark brown sugar

1 cup (200 g) granulated sugar

1 cup (230 g) unsalted butter, melted

4 large eggs

2 tsp (10 ml) vanilla extract

1½ tsp (8 ml) peppermint extract

½ tsp kosher salt

1¼ cups (150 g) all-purpose flour

Crushed peppermint candy, for topping, optional

Preheat the oven to 350°F (180°C). Grease a 9 x 13–inch (22 x 33–cm) pan with butter or nonstick cooking spray and then line the pan with parchment paper, leaving an overhang on all sides. Grease the parchment with butter or nonstick cooking spray and then set it aside.

To a small saucepan, add approximately ½ cup (120 ml) of water and bring it to a boil. In a small bowl, add 1 tablespoon (15 ml) of the boiling water. Add the espresso powder and stir it to combine until a thick liquid or paste forms, then set it aside.

In a large bowl, whisk together the cocoa powder, dark brown sugar and granulated sugar. Add the melted butter and espresso mixture and whisk until combined.

Add the eggs, one at a time, making sure to beat the mixture in between each addition. Then stir in the vanilla and peppermint extracts.

Using a rubber spatula or wooden spoon, fold in the salt and flour until just combined, and then spread the batter evenly into the prepared pan.

Bake for 25 to 30 minutes, sprinkling the crushed peppermint candy, if using, on top of the brownies halfway through baking. Test the brownies with a toothpick inserted into the center of the pan. If it comes out with wet batter, the brownies are not done. If there are only a few moist crumbs, the brownies are done!

Remove the pan from the oven and place it on a wire rack to cool completely in the pan before cutting into squares.

Cover and store leftover brownies in an airtight container at room temperature for 3 to 4 days.

s'mores brownies

What could be more satisfying than roasting a marshmallow to golden perfection over a campfire? Throw some chocolate and graham crackers in, and you've got one of my and America's favorite treats. What? You wish you could roast marshmallows and make s'mores, but you can't? Don't worry, I've got you covered. S'mores Brownies have it all— your favorite homemade brownie, crackly graham crackers and toasty, golden mallows on top. Invite some friends over for a campfire treat in your kitchen—they'll all be begging for s'more! (Sorry, I couldn't resist!)

4½ graham cracker sheets (65 g), plus more for topping

½ cup (60 g) all-purpose flour

1 cup (200 g) sugar

⅓ cup (25 g) unsweetened natural or Dutch-process cocoa powder

¼ tsp kosher salt

¼ tsp baking powder

½ cup (115 g) unsalted butter, melted

2 large eggs

1 tsp vanilla extract

12 large marshmallows, cut into quarters (see Note)

Preheat the oven to 350°F (180°C). Grease an 8 x 8–inch (20 x 20–cm) pan with butter or nonstick cooking spray and then line the pan with parchment paper, leaving an overhang on all sides. Grease the parchment with butter or nonstick cooking spray. Line the graham cracker sheets in an even layer on the bottom of the pan, then set it aside.

In a large bowl, whisk together the flour, sugar, cocoa powder, salt and baking powder.

In a medium bowl, add the butter, eggs and vanilla and whisk until well combined. Add the wet ingredients to the dry ingredients and mix until just combined. Pour the brownie batter into the prepared pan and evenly spread it on top of the graham crackers.

Bake for 30 minutes, then test the brownies by inserting a toothpick into the center of the pan; if it comes out with wet batter, the brownies are not done. If there are only a few moist crumbs, the brownies are done. Keep checking the brownies every 2 minutes until you have moist crumbs.

Remove the pan from the oven and add the marshmallows on top. Return the pan to the top rack of the oven and bake for an additional 2 to 3 minutes, until the marshmallows are melted. Use a culinary torch to further roast the melted marshmallows to your liking, if desired.

Allow the brownies to cool completely before slicing; spraying your knife lightly with cooking spray will help prevent the marshmallow topping from sticking to the blade as you cut.

Cover and store leftover brownies in an airtight container at room temperature for 3 to 4 days.

NOTE: *I find that large marshmallows tend to melt and spread a little better than mini marshmallows. Feel free to use 1 heaping cup (50 g) of mini marshmallows instead, though!*

TOTAL TIME: 1 hour 50 minutes
YIELD: 16 brownies

vanilla bean cheesecake swirl brownies

I think Hannah Montana was talking about these brownies when she said you get the best of both worlds. I mean honestly, the brownie is rich, dense and chocolatey, and swirled into the brownie batter is a simple vanilla bean cheesecake that's distributed throughout so that you get a little bit of creamy cheesecake and chocolate in every bite. Talk about YUM!

VANILLA BEAN CHEESECAKE BATTER

8 oz (225 g) cream cheese, softened

¼ cup (50 g) granulated sugar

1 large egg, at room temperature

1 tsp vanilla bean paste

BROWNIE BATTER

4 oz (115 g) 70% cacao dark chocolate, chopped

¾ cup (170 g) unsalted butter

1 cup (200 g) granulated sugar

½ cup (110 g) dark brown sugar

2 tsp (10 ml) vanilla extract

1 tsp kosher salt

3 large eggs

½ cup (60 g) all-purpose flour

¼ cup (20 g) unsweetened natural or Dutch-process cocoa powder

Preheat the oven to 350°F (180°C). Grease an 8 x 8–inch (20 x 20–cm) pan with butter or nonstick cooking spray and then line the pan with parchment paper, leaving an overhang on all sides. Grease the parchment with butter or nonstick cooking spray and then set it aside.

To make the vanilla bean cheesecake batter, in the bowl of a stand mixer fitted with the paddle attachment, beat the softened cream cheese until smooth and creamy, about 2 minutes. Add the granulated sugar and beat another 2 to 3 minutes. Add the egg and vanilla bean paste and beat until smooth and well combined. Transfer the vanilla bean cheesecake batter to a separate bowl.

To make the brownie batter, place the chopped chocolate in a medium heatproof bowl and set aside. In a small saucepan, heat the butter over medium heat and cook, frequently stirring, just until the butter comes to a vigorous simmer. Immediately pour the hot butter over the chocolate and let it sit for 2 minutes, then whisk until the chocolate is completely smooth and melted. Set it aside.

In the bowl of a stand mixer fitted with the whisk attachment, beat the granulated sugar, dark brown sugar, vanilla, salt and eggs for precisely 10 minutes at high speed. (It will look like a very thick batter.) With the mixer running, pour in the slightly cooled chocolate mixture and beat at medium speed until smooth. Sift in the flour and cocoa powder and use a rubber spatula to gently fold until just combined.

Pour half of the brownie batter into the prepared pan and smooth the top with a spatula. Top with half of the cheesecake batter. Repeat to make one more brownie layer and one more cheesecake layer. With a small spatula or butter knife, gently swirl the two batters to create a marbled effect.

Bake for 45 to 50 minutes. Test the brownies with a toothpick inserted into the center of the pan. If it comes out with wet batter, the brownies are not done. If there are only a few moist crumbs, the brownies are done!

Remove the pan from the oven and place on a wire rack to cool. Allow the brownies to cool completely in the pan. Using the excess parchment as handles, remove the brownies from the pan and cut into 16 squares.

Cover and store leftover brownies in an airtight container at room temperature for 3 to 4 days.

malted chocolate brownies

Malted chocolate isn't just for milkshakes! These Malted Chocolate Brownies have a bit of malted milk powder mixed directly into the batter. I find it provides a subtle roasty, toasty flavor that mellows all the chocolate and sweetness just slightly. Basically, everything you love about a malted chocolate shake in a brownie.

BROWNIES

½ cup (60 g) all-purpose flour

¼ cup (45 g) malted milk powder

1 tbsp (5 g) unsweetened natural or Dutch-process cocoa powder

½ tsp kosher salt

6 tbsp (85 g) unsalted butter

2 oz (60 g) milk chocolate, chopped

2 oz (60 g) 70% cacao dark chocolate, chopped

½ cup (100 g) granulated sugar

½ cup (110 g) light brown sugar

2 large eggs

2 tsp (10 ml) vanilla extract

CHOCOLATE GANACHE

3 oz (85 g) semisweet chocolate, chopped

¼ cup (60 ml) heavy cream

Flaky sea salt, for topping, optional

Preheat the oven to 350°F (180°C). Line an 8 x 8–inch (20 x 20–cm) pan with aluminum foil and spray it with nonstick cooking spray. Set it aside.

In a medium bowl, whisk together the flour, malted milk powder, cocoa powder and salt. Set it aside.

Place the butter and chopped milk and dark chocolates in a heatproof bowl and set it over a pan of gently simmering water to create a double boiler. Stir it occasionally until the chocolate is fully melted. Whisk in the granulated sugar and light brown sugar until thoroughly combined, and then remove from the heat. Whisk in the eggs and vanilla, and then fold in the dry ingredients using a rubber spatula or wooden spoon until just combined.

Pour the batter into the prepared pan and bake for 25 to 30 minutes, until the center is just set.

To make the chocolate ganache, place the chopped chocolate in a medium heatproof bowl. Heat the cream in a small saucepan over medium heat until it begins to simmer gently, about 4 minutes. (Do not let it come to a boil, as that's too hot!) Pour the cream over the chocolate, and then let it sit for 2 to 3 minutes to gently soften the chocolate. With a metal spoon or small rubber spatula, very slowly stir until thoroughly combined and the chocolate has melted. Allow the brownies to cool completely before topping them with the chocolate ganache and flaky sea salt, if using.

Cover and store leftover brownies in an airtight container at room temperature for 3 to 4 days.

NOTE: *The ganache thickens as it cools. Once completely cool and thick (about 2 hours), the ganache can be piped with a piping tip or spread with an offset spatula. You can also beat the cooled, thickened ganache with an electric hand mixer or stand mixer fitted with a whisk attachment until light in color and texture, about 4 minutes on medium-high speed.*

bourbon–pecan brownies

These brownies are delightfully boozy—they're just the right amount of tipsy without crossing the line to sloppy. They're rich but surprisingly delicate and a little fudgy, with good crumb and a crisp, almost meringue-like top. For a deep flavor, use premium bourbon like Maker's Mark or even a high-quality whiskey like Jack Daniel's Black Label.

¼ cup (30 g) all-purpose flour

⅓ cup (25 g) unsweetened natural or Dutch-process cocoa powder

¼ tsp baking powder

¼ tsp instant espresso powder

½ tsp kosher salt

½ cup (115 g) unsalted butter, cut into cubes

5 oz (140 g) 70–75% cacao dark or bittersweet chocolate, finely chopped

1 cup (200 g) granulated sugar

2 large eggs

3 tbsp (45 ml) bourbon

¾ cup (85 g) coarsely chopped pecans, divided

Flaky sea salt, for topping, optional

Preheat the oven to 350°F (180°C). Grease an 8 x 8–inch (20 x 20–cm) pan with butter or nonstick cooking spray and then line the pan with parchment paper, leaving an overhang on all sides. Grease the parchment with butter or nonstick cooking spray and then set it aside.

In a medium bowl, whisk together the flour, cocoa powder, baking powder, espresso powder and salt. Set it aside.

In a saucepan, combine the butter and chopped chocolate. Stir over low heat until the chocolate is almost melted. Remove from the heat and continue to gently stir until smooth; the residual heat from the pan should be enough to melt the last few bits of chocolate.

Whisk in the granulated sugar until incorporated; the batter will be slightly grainy and paste-like.

Whisk in the eggs, one at a time, whisking completely after each one until the batter is smooth and shiny. Whisk in the bourbon.

Add the dry ingredients and stir until just incorporated. Stir in ½ cup (55 g) of pecans. Spread the batter into the prepared pan, using an offset spatula to smooth the batter into the corners. Sprinkle the top with the remaining ¼ cup (30 g) of pecans.

Bake for 25 to 30 minutes, or until the top is shiny and crackly and a toothpick inserted near the center comes out mostly clean. Top with flaky sea salt, if using, after baking. Allow the brownies to cool in the pan on a wire rack before slicing into squares.

Cover and store leftover brownies in an airtight container at room temperature for 3 to 4 days.

nutella® brownies

These Nutella® Brownies almost didn't happen, but I'm glad they did. They were a late-night, "Oh hey, chocolate sounds kinda good, let's make brownies" experiment. As I was grabbing the flour from my cabinet, I bumped into the jar of Nutella and, well, I just went with it. Divine intervention, y'all, it's a thing. These brownies are a must-try for all Nutella lovers, because they are chock-full of that delicious chocolate-hazelnut flavor and not much else!

6 tbsp (85 g) unsalted butter, melted

½ cup (110 g) light brown sugar

2 large eggs

2 tsp (10 ml) vanilla extract

1¼ cups (370 g) Nutella, divided

½ tsp kosher salt

⅔ cup (80 g) all-purpose flour

½ cup (85 g) semisweet chocolate chips

Flaky sea salt, to taste

Preheat the oven to 350°F (180°C). Grease an 8 x 8–inch (20 x 20–cm) pan with butter or nonstick cooking spray and then line the pan with parchment paper, leaving an overhang on all sides. Grease the parchment with butter or nonstick cooking spray and then set it aside.

In a medium bowl, whisk together the melted butter and light brown sugar until combined. Add the eggs and vanilla. Beat until combined.

Add in 1 cup (296 g) of the Nutella and the salt. Mix until smooth and fluffy, about 3 to 4 minutes, scraping down the sides of the bowl as needed.

Add the flour and mix until just combined. The batter will be thick. Using a rubber spatula, fold in the chocolate chips.

Pour the batter into the prepared pan. Drop teaspoonfuls of the remaining ¼ cup (74 g) of Nutella along the top. Using a knife, swirl the spread into the batter. Top with a sprinkle of flaky sea salt.

Bake for 30 to 35 minutes. Test the brownies with a toothpick inserted into the center of the pan. If it comes out with wet batter, the brownies are not done. If there are only a few moist crumbs, the brownies are done. Be careful not to overbake!

Remove the pan from the oven and set it on a wire rack to cool. When cool, carefully lift the parchment paper out of the pan and cut the brownies into squares.

Cover and store leftover brownies in an airtight container at room temperature for 3 to 4 days.

dulce de leche brownies

For those of you who might not be familiar with dulce de leche, it's basically a sweetened milk caramel; it's like caramel, but creamier. And when marbled inside of these brownies, it's even more irresistible. These brownies are great cold or at room temperature—or heat them for a few seconds in the microwave and you'll get little melty pools of dulce de leche when you break into them. Can you say heaven?!

½ cup (115 g) unsalted butter

¾ cup (60 g) unsweetened natural or Dutch-process cocoa powder

¾ cup (150 g) granulated sugar

½ cup (110 g) dark brown sugar

½ tbsp (8 ml) vanilla extract

2 large eggs

½ tsp kosher salt

½ tsp baking powder

½ cup (60 g) all-purpose flour

½ cup (120 ml) dulce de leche, divided (see Note)

Preheat the oven to 350°F (180°C). Grease an 8 x 8–inch (20 x 20–cm) pan with butter or nonstick cooking spray and then line the pan with parchment paper, leaving an overhang on all sides. Grease the parchment with butter or nonstick cooking spray and then set it aside.

In a saucepan, melt the butter over medium-low heat until it's completely melted. Add the cocoa powder, granulated sugar and dark brown sugar and stir very well. Allow to cool for about 3 minutes before continuing.

Add the vanilla, then the eggs one at a time, beating between each addition. Add the salt, baking powder and flour and stir until just combined and there are no more patches of flour.

Spread about half of the batter into the prepared pan and drop ¼ cup (60 ml) of the dulce de leche on top in dollops before swirling lightly with a toothpick or knife. Top with the remaining batter and the remaining dulce de leche and swirl again slightly.

Bake the brownies for 27 to 30 minutes, or until a toothpick inserted in the center comes out clean of batter. Allow the brownies to cool completely in the pan before cutting into bars.

Cover and store leftover brownies in an airtight container at room temperature for 3 to 4 days.

NOTE: *These brownies will work with either store-bought or homemade dulce de leche. For a semi-homemade version of dulce de leche, completely submerge a 14-ounce (420-ml) can of sweetened condensed milk in a large saucepan of simmering water for 2 to 3 hours, refilling the pan with boiling water as needed to keep the can submerged; allow to cool completely on a wire rack before attempting to open the can since the contents will be hot and under pressure!*

kitchen sink brownies

Not only are these brownies quick and straightforward to make, but they're also delicious and infinitely customizable. More appropriately titled "everything but the kitchen sink brownies," this brownie recipe is a great base to work from and allows you to customize your own toppings.

BROWNIES

½ cup (115 g) unsalted butter

1 cup (175 g) semisweet chocolate chips, divided

¾ cup (150 g) granulated sugar

½ tbsp (8 ml) vanilla extract

1 tsp espresso powder

2 large eggs

¼ cup (30 g) all-purpose flour

¼ cup (20 g) unsweetened natural or Dutch-process cocoa powder

1 tsp baking powder

TOPPING

4 oz (115 g) 70% cacao dark chocolate, chopped

3 tbsp (43 g) unsalted butter

¼ cup (20 g) pretzels, chopped

¼ cup (9 g) potato chips, chopped

¼ cup (25 g) chopped cream-filled chocolate sandwich cookies (I like Oreos®)

¼ cup (85 g) chopped peanut butter cups

Preheat the oven to 350°F (180°C). Grease an 8 x 8–inch (20 x 20–cm) pan with butter or nonstick cooking spray and then line the pan with parchment paper, leaving an overhang on all sides. Grease the parchment with butter or nonstick cooking spray and then set it aside.

To make the brownies, in the microwave, melt together the butter and ¾ cup (130 g) of chocolate chips in a medium microwave-safe bowl, stirring at 30-second intervals, until melted and smooth. Stir in the sugar, vanilla and espresso powder.

Beat the eggs, one at a time, into the chocolate mix. Add the flour, cocoa powder and baking powder. Stir until just combined. Stir in the remaining ¼ cup (45 g) of chocolate chips.

Evenly spread the mixture into the prepared pan. Bake for 28 to 30 minutes, or until the brownies are just set.

To make the topping, in a small microwave-safe bowl, melt and stir together the chopped chocolate and butter in the microwave until smooth. Pour the mixture over the top of the warm brownies and then sprinkle the chopped pretzels, potato chips, cookies and peanut butter cups on top. Let the brownies cool completely before slicing.

Cover and store leftover brownies in an airtight container at room temperature for 3 to 4 days.

NOTE: *These brownies can be topped with any of your favorite snacks— just make sure you don't add more than 1 cup (240 g) of chopped toppings! Some of my other favorite toppings include M&M'S®, peanuts, yogurt-covered pretzels and toasted coconut.*

TOTAL TIME: 1 hour 30 minutes
YIELD: 18 ice cream sandwiches

brownie ice cream sandwiches

Sweet baby Jesus, where have these been my whole life? The brownie is chewy and exceptionally flavorful due to the use of light brown sugar, unsweetened cocoa and black cocoa. And even when eaten straight from the freezer, the brownies are surprisingly soft. My favorite ice creams for these brownie sandwiches are cookies 'n' cream (pictured here) or vanilla bean, but I encourage experimentation!

BROWNIES

3 oz (85 g) 70% cacao dark chocolate, roughly chopped

½ cup (115 g) unsalted butter

½ cup (100 g) granulated sugar

½ cup (110 g) light brown sugar

2 large eggs

1 tsp vanilla extract

½ tsp kosher salt

¼ tsp ground cinnamon

⅔ cup (80 g) all-purpose flour

1 tbsp (5 g) black cocoa powder

1 tbsp (5 g) unsweetened natural or Dutch-process cocoa powder

FILLING

2 cups (475 g) ice cream of your choice, softened

Preheat the oven to 350°F (180°C). Line two 8 x 8–inch (20 x 20–cm) pans with parchment paper, extending it up two sides of each pan. Grease the parchment paper and exposed sides of the pan with butter or spray them with a nonstick cooking spray. Set them aside.

To make the brownies, in a medium heatproof bowl placed over gently simmering water, heat the chocolate and butter together until melted. Remove from the heat and stir until smooth. Once the chocolate mixture has slightly cooled, stir in the granulated sugar and light brown sugar until thoroughly combined, then whisk in the eggs, one at a time. Stir in the vanilla. Stir in the salt and the cinnamon until combined, then mix in the flour and black and unsweetened cocoa powders until just combined.

Divide the batter between the two prepared pans and spread it evenly using an offset spatula. This recipe makes around 24 ounces (680 g) of batter; pour 12 ounces (340 g) into each pan to ensure even layers and then bake on different racks for 13 to 15 minutes, switching the pans top-to-bottom halfway through baking and rotating the pans as you switch.

Transfer the hot pans directly to the freezer (you can put down dish towels or a cooling rack to protect the shelves). Chill until cold and firm, about 15 to 20 minutes.

Remove the first pan from the freezer and cover it with ice cream. Use an offset spatula to smoosh down the ice cream and smooth the top. Remove the second brownie pan from the freezer, remove the parchment, and place the brownies upside down on top of the ice cream. Place the empty brownie pan on top of the brownie sandwiches to weigh it down. Press down a little. Keeping the extra pan on top, return the brownie–ice cream stack to the freezer until sufficiently firm, another 30 minutes.

Run a knife around the brownie stack again to make sure it's not stuck and use the parchment sling to transfer the ice cream sandwich block to a cutting board to cut into squares.

You can store the cut sandwiches in an airtight container or bag in the freezer as is or individually wrapped in squares of waxed paper. They should keep for at least one month in the freezer, but good luck keeping them that long!

small-batch brownies

These Small-Batch Brownies are going to change your life. They're magnificently fudgy and chewy and chocolatey. And because they're made in a loaf pan, they make a modest number rather than an entire panful; just enough to share with those you love most in the world, with none left over to tempt you the rest of the week. Or just enough to devour on your own because they're small-batch, and that's acceptable, right!?

6 tbsp (85 g) unsalted butter, cubed
6 tbsp (75 g) granulated sugar
6 tbsp (80 g) light brown sugar
¼ cup (20 g) unsweetened natural cocoa powder
½ tsp vanilla extract
1 tsp water
1 large egg
¼ cup (30 g) all-purpose flour
¼ tsp baking soda
Pinch of kosher salt

Preheat the oven to 350°F (180°C). Grease a 9 x 5–inch (22 x 13–cm) loaf pan with butter or nonstick cooking spray or line the inside with aluminum foil, leaving a couple inches of overhang. If using foil, spray it with nonstick cooking spray or grease it with butter. Set the pan aside.

Place the butter in a light-colored skillet. (A light-colored skillet will help you determine when the butter begins browning.) Melt the butter over medium heat, stirring constantly. Once melted, the butter will start to foam. Keep stirring. After 5 to 8 minutes, the butter will begin browning; you'll notice lightly browned specks begin to form at the bottom of the pan, and you'll start to smell a nutty aroma.

Once the butter is browned, immediately remove it from the heat, pour it into a medium heatproof mixing bowl and stir in the granulated sugar, light brown sugar, cocoa powder, vanilla and water. Stir until well combined. Set it aside for about 5 minutes to cool slightly (this prevents the egg from cooking once it is added to the batter).

After 5 minutes, add the egg and beat well until combined. Then add the flour, baking soda and salt and stir vigorously for about 1 minute.

Pour the batter into the prepared loaf pan. Bake for 20 to 22 minutes, until the tops of the brownies appear dry and a toothpick inserted into the center comes out relatively clean (there might be a little chocolate clinging to it; that's fine as long as it's crumbs and not batter). Allow the brownies to cool slightly before removing them from the pan and cutting them.

Cover and store leftover brownies in an airtight container at room temperature for 3 to 4 days.

gluten-free almond flour brownies

When making a dessert for an unfamiliar crowd, it can be a stressful challenge to bake something that 1) tastes great, 2) won't take half your day and a counter full of ingredients to prepare and 3) can be enjoyed by nearly everyone, including people on special diets. That's where these Almond Flour Brownies come in—delicious, easy to make (read: one bowl) and enjoyable by those on both gluten-free and grain-free diets!

6 tbsp (85 g) unsalted butter, melted

1 cup (200 g) granulated sugar

¾ cup (165 g) dark brown sugar

½ tsp kosher salt

¾ cup (60 g) unsweetened natural or Dutch-process cocoa powder

1 tsp vanilla extract

3 large eggs

1½ cups (145 g) almond flour

1 tsp baking powder

Flaky sea salt, for topping, optional

Preheat the oven to 350°F (180°C). Grease an 8 x 8–inch (20 x 20–cm) loaf pan with butter or nonstick cooking spray or line the inside with aluminum foil, leaving a couple inches of overhang. If using foil, spray it with nonstick cooking spray or grease it with butter. Set the pan aside.

In a large bowl, whisk together the butter, granulated sugar, dark brown sugar, salt and cocoa powder until well combined. Add the vanilla and then the eggs, one at a time, beating between each addition.

Add the almond flour and baking powder and stir until combined. The batter will be thick and fairly smooth, showing only a slight graininess from the almond flour.

Scoop the batter into the prepared pan and bake for 35 to 37 minutes. When they're done, the top of the brownies should look set, and when you shake the pan slightly, the center shouldn't jiggle. Top with flaky sea salt, if using, after baking. Allow the brownies to cool before removing from the pan and cutting them.

Cover and store leftover brownies in an airtight container at room temperature for 3 to 4 days.

bakery-style brownies

There are two secrets to this brownie recipe; first, the powdered sugar in place of regular granulated sugar, which gives these brownies a dense, fudgy texture. Second, the cocoa powder is "bloomed," which means that the cocoa is added to a warm liquid—in this case, oil—stirred until it is lump-free and then set aside to sit for a few minutes. The cocoa dissolves and becomes fragrant, making for an insanely delicious brownie reminiscent of your favorite bakery. A word of advice: use a hand mixer for this recipe as the chocolate-oil mixture needs to emulsify; once well mixed, it will bake up as smooth and tasty as can be.

⅔ cup (160 ml) canola oil

⅔ cup (50 g) unsweetened natural or Dutch-process cocoa powder

½ cup (60 g) all-purpose flour

¼ tsp baking powder

½ tsp kosher salt

3 large eggs

1⅓ cups (160 g) powdered sugar, plus more for topping, optional

⅔ cup (150 g) dark brown sugar

1 tsp vanilla extract

Arrange a rack in the middle of the oven and preheat the oven to 325°F (160°C). Coat a 9 x 9–inch (22 x 22–cm) pan with nonstick cooking spray and set it aside.

Place the oil into a medium microwave-safe bowl and heat on low power in 5-second bursts four to six times until the oil is warm but not hot. Add the cocoa powder and whisk until completely smooth and combined. Let sit for 4 to 5 minutes so the cocoa can bloom. Meanwhile, prepare the dry and wet ingredients.

In a small bowl, whisk the flour, baking powder and salt to combine; set aside.

In the bowl of a stand mixer fitted with the paddle attachment, or in a large bowl using an electric hand mixer, beat the eggs, powdered sugar and dark brown sugar on medium speed until fluffy and lighter in color, 3 to 4 minutes. Beat in the vanilla until just combined.

Add the cocoa mixture to the egg mixture and mix at medium-high speed until shiny and fully combined, about 5 minutes. Add the flour mixture to the egg and cocoa mixture and mix at low speed until fully combined. Transfer to the prepared pan and spread the batter into an even layer.

Bake for 20 to 24 minutes (you can bake for up to 30 minutes if you like a firmer brownie with some crisp edges). The brownies will pull away from the edges of the pan, but a cake tester or knife inserted in the middle will not come out clean. Let cool completely before dusting with powdered sugar, if using, and cutting into 16 squares.

Cover and store leftover brownies in an airtight container at room temperature for 3 to 4 days.

cookies 'n' cream brownies

These Cookies 'n' Cream Brownies are perfect for the Oreo lover. They're super dark and rich and easy to bake up! These brownies start with a fudgy brownie base and are slathered with a creamy Oreo white-chocolate frosting. Talk about the perfect dessert to wow someone!

BROWNIE LAYER

6 tbsp (85 g) unsalted butter

2 oz (60 g) 70% cacao dark chocolate, chopped

1 cup (200 g) granulated sugar

2 large eggs

1 tsp vanilla extract

½ cup (40 g) unsweetened natural or Dutch-process cocoa powder

1 tbsp (5 g) black cocoa powder

½ cup (60 g) all-purpose flour

½ tsp kosher salt

1 cup (100 g) chopped cream-filled chocolate sandwich cookies, approximately 7 cookies (I like Oreos®)

COOKIES 'N' CREAM LAYER

6 oz (170 g) white chocolate, chopped

3 tbsp (45 ml) heavy whipping cream

2 tbsp (16 g) powdered sugar

¾ cup (75 g) chopped cream-filled chocolate sandwich cookies, approximately 5 cookies

Preheat the oven to 350°F (180°C). Grease an 8 x 8–inch (20 x 20–cm) pan with butter or nonstick cooking spray and then line the pan with parchment paper, leaving an overhang on all sides. Grease the parchment with butter or nonstick cooking spray and then set it aside.

To make the brownies, place the butter and chopped chocolate in a heatproof bowl and set over a pan of gently simmering water to create a double boiler. Stir occasionally until the chocolate is fully melted. Remove the bowl from the heat and whisk in the sugar until completely combined. Allow to cool slightly.

Whisk in the eggs and vanilla until well combined. Then fold in the cocoa powder, black cocoa powder, flour and salt using a rubber spatula or wooden spoon. Fold in the chopped cookies until combined and then spread the batter evenly into the prepared pan.

Bake for 25 to 30 minutes. Test the brownies with a toothpick inserted into the center of the pan. If it comes out with wet batter, the brownies are not done. If there are only a few moist crumbs, the brownies are done. Keep checking every 2 minutes until you have moist crumbs.

Remove from the oven and place on a wire rack to cool completely.

Once the brownies are mostly cool, make the cookies 'n' cream layer.

To make the cookies 'n' cream layer, in a microwave-safe bowl, add the chopped white chocolate and heavy whipping cream. Heat in 20- to 30-second increments, stirring well after each, until melted and smooth, about 2 minutes. Stir in the powdered sugar and chopped cookies, then spread the mixture evenly on top of the brownies. The mixture will be thick, so use an offset spatula to help spread it.

Cover and store leftover brownies in an airtight container at room temperature for 3 to 4 days.

red velvet brownies

When it comes to these Red Velvet Brownies, you really can't go wrong. They have a deliciously fudgy, chewy texture with a mild chocolate flavor, slight tanginess and beautiful red hue. Not to mention the creamy cream cheese frosting that makes them extra drool-worthy. Add these to the top of your "to-bake" list!

BROWNIES

1 cup (120 g) all-purpose flour

½ tsp baking powder

¼ tsp salt

2 oz (60 g) 70% cacao dark chocolate, chopped

½ cup (115 g) unsalted butter

1 cup (200 g) granulated sugar

¼ cup (55 g) light brown sugar

1 tbsp (15 ml) red food coloring

2 tsp (10 ml) vanilla extract

1 tsp apple cider vinegar

2 large eggs

CREAM CHEESE FROSTING

½ cup (115 g) butter, softened

4 oz (113 g) cream cheese, softened

2½ cups (300 g) powdered sugar

½ tsp vanilla bean paste

Pinch of salt, to taste

Preheat the oven to 350°F (180°C). Grease an 8 x 8–inch (20 x 20–cm) pan with butter or nonstick cooking spray and then line the pan with parchment paper, leaving an overhang on all sides. Grease the parchment with butter or nonstick cooking spray and then set it aside.

To make the brownies, in a mixing bowl, whisk together the flour, baking powder and salt, and set it aside.

To a large microwave-safe bowl, add the chopped chocolate and butter and heat the mixture in the microwave on 50% power, in 30-second intervals, stirring after each interval until the chocolate is melted and smooth (alternately you can melt it in a double boiler over the stove top).

Add the granulated sugar and light brown sugar to the melted chocolate mixture, and, using a rubber spatula, stir to combine.

Mix in the red food coloring, vanilla and apple cider vinegar. Stir in the eggs. Add the flour mixture and mix just until combined.

Pour the batter into the prepared pan, spread into an even layer and bake for 35 to 40 minutes, until a toothpick comes out with a few moist crumbs. Place the pan on a wire rack to cool the brownies completely.

To make the cream cheese frosting, in a large bowl using a handheld mixer, beat the butter and cream cheese together on high speed until they're smooth and creamy. Add the powdered sugar, vanilla bean paste and salt. Beat on low speed for 30 seconds, then switch to high speed and beat for 2 minutes. Add a pinch of salt if the frosting is too sweet. (I usually add anywhere between ⅛ to ¼ teaspoon of salt.)

Remove the cooled brownies from the pan and frost the bars with a thick layer of the frosting before cutting into squares.

Cover and store leftover brownies in an airtight container at room temperature for 1 day or in the refrigerator for 3 days.

TOTAL TIME: 1 hour 30 minutes
YIELD: 24 brownies

chocolate chip cookie brownies

Brownies and chocolate chip cookies are timeless dessert classics. This recipe takes both components and bakes them into one ultra-rich and satisfying dessert. They're the ultimate treat for the chocolate lover who refuses to choose between chocolate chip cookies and brownies. It's an obvious win-win!

COOKIE DOUGH (SEE NOTE)

½ cup (115 g) unsalted butter, softened

½ cup (100 g) granulated sugar

¼ cup (55 g) dark brown sugar

1 egg

½ tsp vanilla extract

1 cup + 2 tbsp (135 g) all-purpose flour

½ tsp baking soda

½ tsp salt

1 cup (175 g) semisweet chocolate chips

BROWNIES

1 cup (230 g) unsalted butter

12 oz (340 g) 60% cacao semisweet chocolate, chopped

1½ cups (330 g) light brown sugar

1 tbsp (15 ml) vanilla extract

4 large eggs

½ cup (60 g) all-purpose flour

½ cup (40 g) unsweetened natural or Dutch-process cocoa powder

2 tsp (10 g) baking powder

Preheat the oven to 350°F (180°C). Grease a 9 x 13–inch (22 x 33–cm) pan with butter or nonstick cooking spray and then line the pan with parchment paper, leaving an overhang on all sides. Grease the parchment with butter or nonstick cooking spray and then set it aside.

To make the cookie dough, in a medium bowl, use an electric hand mixer to cream together the butter, granulated sugar and dark brown sugar for 4 to 5 minutes. Add the egg and vanilla and cream again until smooth. Next, stir in the flour, baking soda, salt and chocolate chips with a rubber spatula or wooden spoon until fully combined. Set aside in the refrigerator.

To make the brownies, in a medium microwave-safe bowl, melt together the butter and chopped chocolate in the microwave, stirring at 30-second intervals, until the chocolate is melted and smooth. Stir in the light brown sugar and vanilla.

In a small bowl, whisk the eggs for 1 minute until they're bubbly on top. Stir the eggs into the chocolate mixture. Add the flour, cocoa powder and baking powder and stir until just combined.

Evenly spread the brownie mixture into the prepared pan. Scatter pieces of cookie dough over the top of the brownie batter; you will have cookie dough left over (see Note). Bake for 40 to 45 minutes, or until the brownies are just set; cover the brownies loosely with aluminum foil if the cookies are browning too quickly. Let cool completely before slicing.

Cover and store leftover brownies in an airtight container at room temperature for 3 to 4 days.

NOTE: *You will have more cookie dough than you need for this recipe! Only about two-thirds of the dough will fit into the pan. Cover and refrigerate the extra dough to bake as traditional cookies in a 350°F (180°C) preheated oven for 11 to 12 minutes.*

white chocolate brownies

Some of you are probably thinking, "But wait, isn't a white chocolate brownie just a blondie?" No, not at all! Blondies aren't made with white chocolate as the base (more on this in the next chapter). So, you're in for a real treat with these; we'll call them the fudge brownie's not-so-innocent twin.

½ cup (115 g) unsalted butter

3 oz (85 g) white chocolate, chopped (see Note)

¾ cup (150 g) granulated sugar

2 large eggs

1 tsp vanilla extract

¾ cup (90 g) all-purpose flour

½ tsp kosher salt

½ cup (90 g) white chocolate chips, optional

Preheat the oven to 350°F (180°C). Grease an 8 x 8–inch (20 x 20–cm) pan with butter or nonstick cooking spray and then line the pan with parchment paper, leaving an overhang on all sides. Grease the parchment with butter or nonstick cooking spray and then set it aside.

Place the butter and chopped white chocolate in a heatproof bowl and set over a pan of gently simmering water to create a double boiler. Stir occasionally until the chocolate is fully melted. Remove the bowl from the heat and whisk in the sugar until completely combined. Allow the mixture to cool slightly.

Whisk in the eggs and vanilla until well combined. Then fold in the flour and salt using a rubber spatula or wooden spoon. If using, fold in the white chocolate chips until combined. The batter will be thick. Spread it evenly into the prepared pan.

Bake for 30 minutes, covering loosely with aluminum foil halfway through. Test the brownies with a toothpick at the 30-minute mark. Insert it into the center of the pan; if it comes out with wet batter, the brownies are not done. If there are only a few moist crumbs, the brownies are done. Keep checking every 2 minutes until you have moist crumbs.

Remove the pan from the oven and place it on a wire rack to cool completely.

Cover and store leftover brownies in an airtight container at room temperature for 3 to 4 days.

NOTE: *Be sure to use a high-quality white chocolate bar or feves. White baking chips usually don't contain any cocoa butter, which is needed for this recipe, but they make great add-ins!*

blondies have more fun

I'm here to let you in on a little secret that not many people know: blondies came before brownies. Yep, you read that right. A lot of people think of blondies as brownies without chocolate, as if blondies were just an afterthought, a simplification of the original, but that's not the case!

Despite predating it by at least 10 years, the blondie has never enjoyed the same chart-topping success as its darker cousin. The first brownie recipes popped up in the late 1800s. Still, chocolate didn't make an appearance until 1906. Up until that point, the brownie was a dense, fudgy, butterscotch-flavored bar known to us modern folks as the blondie.

A blondie is like a brownie, except it's based on brown sugar instead of cocoa. This results in a taste that's reminiscent of butterscotch rather than the familiar chocolatey flavor we all know and love. The best thing about blondies (aside from their melt-in-your-mouth gooey centers, of course) is how easy they are to make. There's no melting down chocolate or sifting pesky cocoa powder. All you need are a few basic kitchen tools, a short list of everyday ingredients and an hour. For such minimal effort, the rewards are ridiculous.

While I absolutely adore brownies, I wholeheartedly believe blondies are terribly underrated, and so I'm here to help change that. If ever there were a blondie recipe to start with, it's the Birthday Cake Blondies (page 59). Just trust me and prepare to be amazed.

Let's have some fun, shall we?!

TIPS & TECHNIQUES

- Always line your baking pan. Eating blondies is fun; cleaning up after them isn't. The solution? Line your pan with aluminum foil or parchment paper. This not only makes for easy cleanup, but it also keeps the blondies from sticking to the pan. Talk about a win-win.

- Temperature matters. Yes, you're going to need to melt your butter. But don't combine screaming hot, just-melted butter to your eggs and sugar—we do not want scrambled eggs here. Also, be sure to bring your eggs to room temperature before combining. Does it take a little planning to remove those eggs from the fridge an hour in advance? Sure, but they'll combine much better than when cold, yielding a smoother, creamier batter.

- If you forget to take your ingredients out of the fridge before beginning, or you have a spur-of-the-moment sweet tooth craving that needs satisfying ASAP, stick your ingredients in warm (not hot!) water for about 15 minutes.

- Don't overmix your batter. You've no doubt been told at one time or another not to do this, but do you know why? Sure, all the ingredients need to be well incorporated, which includes taking a spatula and scraping the stuff that sticks to the side of the mixing bowl. But get too crazy with it and you risk developing too much gluten in the flour, which will change the structure of the blondie (or any baked good for that matter). When you overmix, you wind up with stiff and dense (in a bad way) blondies.

birthday cake blondies

If you make these delightful little Birthday Cake Blondies, be prepared to take a nibble and then go far, far away from them. I didn't think temptation would come in the form of thin, white chocolate and sprinkled blondie bars; however, I was completely proven wrong. I literally couldn't stop sneaking nibbles, bites and entire quadrants of these blondies; their simplicity is what won me over, and I'm sure they'll steal your heart too!

1½ cups (180 g) all-purpose flour

½ tsp kosher salt

1 tsp baking powder

½ cup (115 g) unsalted butter, melted

¾ cup (165 g) dark brown sugar

½ cup (100 g) granulated sugar

2 large eggs

1 tbsp (15 ml) clear imitation vanilla extract (see Note)

6 tbsp (60 g) rainbow sprinkles, divided

½ cup (90 g) white chocolate chips, divided

Preheat the oven to 350°F (180°C). Grease an 8 x 8–inch (20 x 20–cm) pan with butter or nonstick cooking spray and then line the pan with parchment paper, leaving an overhang on all sides. Grease the parchment with butter or nonstick cooking spray and then set it aside.

In a medium bowl, combine the flour, salt and baking powder. Set aside.

In a large bowl, whisk the melted butter, dark brown sugar and granulated sugar together for about a minute. Add the eggs and vanilla and beat until lighter in color, about 4 minutes. Gradually add the dry ingredients to the wet ingredients and mix until just combined.

Gently fold in 4 tablespoons (40 g) of the sprinkles and ¼ cup (45 g) of the white chocolate chips until evenly incorporated. Transfer the batter to the pan and top with the remaining ¼ cup (45 g) of white chocolate chips and the remaining 2 tablespoons (20 g) of sprinkles.

Bake until the top and edges are set and golden, 30 to 35 minutes. Remove from the oven and allow the blondies to cool in the pan for 45 minutes before removing and slicing.

Cover and store leftover blondies in an airtight container at room temperature for 2 to 3 days.

NOTE: *I learned this trick from Milk Bar years ago—clear imitation vanilla extract is what gives you the funfetti birthday cake flavor from your childhood. You can replace it with 1 tablespoon (15 ml) of pure vanilla extract if that's all you have!*

TOTAL TIME: 1 hour 20 minutes
YIELD: 16 bars

cinnamon roll blondies

There aren't many things that can't be improved with cream cheese. Or, at least that is my philosophy! I really wanted to make a fun dessert with the flavors of cinnamon rolls without having to go through the trouble of making them from scratch. And thus, Cinnamon Roll Blondies were born!

BLONDIES

½ cup (115 g) unsalted butter, cubed

½ cup (110 g) light brown sugar

½ cup (100 g) granulated sugar

1 tsp vanilla extract

2 large eggs

1¼ cups (150 g) all-purpose flour

1 tsp baking powder

½ tsp ground cinnamon

¾ tsp kosher salt

CINNAMON SWIRL

¼ cup (55 g) dark brown sugar

1 tbsp (6 g) ground cinnamon

CREAM CHEESE ICING

1 oz (28 g) cream cheese, softened

1 tbsp (15 g) unsalted butter, softened

¾ cup (90 g) powdered sugar

1½ tbsp (23 ml) milk

½ tsp vanilla bean paste

Preheat the oven to 350°F (180°C). Grease an 8 x 8–inch (20 x 20–cm) pan with butter or nonstick cooking spray and then line the pan with parchment paper, leaving an overhang on all sides. Grease the parchment with butter or nonstick cooking spray and then set it aside.

To make the blondies, place the butter in a light-colored skillet. (The light-colored skillet will help you determine when the butter begins browning.) Melt the butter over medium heat, stirring constantly. Once melted, the butter will start to foam. Keep stirring. After 5 to 8 minutes, the butter will begin browning; you'll notice lightly browned specks begin to form at the bottom of the pan and you'll start to smell a nutty aroma. Once browned, immediately remove from the heat, pour into a large heatproof mixing bowl and let cool slightly.

Once the brown butter has cooled slightly, add the light brown sugar and granulated sugar and whisk. Add the vanilla, followed by the eggs, one at a time, beating between each addition.

Add the flour, baking powder, cinnamon and salt, and stir until just combined. Transfer half of the batter to the prepared pan, spreading it in an even layer.

To make the cinnamon swirl, in a small bowl, stir the dark brown sugar and cinnamon together. Drop large spoonfuls of the cinnamon-sugar mixture on top of the blondie batter, then top it with the remaining batter.

Bake for 30 to 35 minutes, or until the blondies are golden brown and set around the edges. (The middle will look a little doughy, but they will continue to cook as they cool!)

To make the cream cheese icing, in a medium bowl, beat the cream cheese and butter together until smooth and combined, then beat in the powdered sugar, milk and vanilla bean paste.

Once the blondies are cool, drizzle them with the cream cheese icing before cutting into bars.

Cover and store leftover blondies in an airtight container at room temperature for 2 to 3 days.

chocolate chunk tahini blondies

I'm taking your traditional blondie to a whole new level, featuring one of my favorite ingredients: tahini! This recipe is adapted from my dear friend Sarah Fennel, who's also a baking blogger. I had been following Sarah on Instagram for a while, but we met for the first time while we were on a pastry tour together in Israel. That trip was the first time I ever tried tahini, and it was love at first taste.

Tahini (sesame seed paste) is a staple of Middle Eastern and Mediterranean cooking. It's perhaps most notable for its essential role in making hummus, although its uses go far beyond that iconic dip. The tahini in these blondies adds such a pleasant nutty flavor, cutting the sweetness and creating a rich texture.

½ cup (115 g) salted butter, melted

½ cup (130 g) tahini

½ cup (110 g) light brown sugar

½ cup (100 g) granulated sugar

1 large egg

2 tsp (10 ml) vanilla extract

1 cup (120 g) all-purpose flour

½ tsp salt

½ tsp baking soda

6 oz (170 g) 70% cacao dark chocolate, chopped, divided

Preheat the oven to 350°F (180°C). Grease an 8 x 8–inch (20 x 20–cm) pan with butter or nonstick cooking spray and then line the pan with parchment paper, leaving an overhang on all sides. Grease the parchment with butter or nonstick cooking spray and then set it aside.

In a medium bowl, whisk together the melted butter, tahini, light brown sugar and granulated sugar until well combined and fluffy. Add in the egg and vanilla and whisk to combine.

Add the flour, salt and baking soda and stir until just combined. Stir in the chopped chocolate, setting a handful aside for topping.

Pour the batter into the prepared pan and spread it out evenly using a spatula. Top with the remaining chocolate chunks and bake for 30 minutes; the center will look a little under-baked and the edges will be slightly puffed, firm and golden brown.

Let the blondies cool completely in the pan before slicing and serving.

Cover and store leftover blondies in an airtight container at room temperature for 2 to 3 days.

chocolate peanut butter pretzel blondies

I have a confession to make. I'm a bit of a peanut butter hoarder. Actually, all nut butters in general. But at any given time, I probably have at LEAST five jars of different types of peanut butter, and so it's only natural that I include the deliciously sticky spread in baked goods whenever possible. If there was ever a peanut butter dessert recipe to have in your back pocket, it should be these blondies. In fact, I should really be calling these Back-Pocket Chocolate Peanut Butter Pretzel Blondies, but I feel like that title might be a little on the long side. The point is, these are the best blondies. Try them for yourself!

½ cup (115 g) unsalted butter, melted

4 tbsp (64 g) creamy peanut butter, divided

½ cup (110 g) light brown sugar

¼ cup (50 g) granulated sugar

1 large egg

½ tbsp (8 ml) vanilla extract

1 cup (120 g) all-purpose flour

½ tsp baking powder

¾ cup (130 g) semisweet chocolate chips

16 mini pretzels

Flaky sea salt, optional

Preheat the oven to 350°F (180°C). Grease an 8 x 8–inch (20 x 20–cm) pan with butter or nonstick cooking spray and then line the pan with parchment paper, leaving an overhang on all sides. Grease the parchment with butter or nonstick cooking spray and then set it aside.

In a large bowl, thoroughly combine the melted butter, 2 tablespoons (32 g) of peanut butter, the light brown sugar and granulated sugar. Add the egg and vanilla and beat until incorporated. Then add the flour and baking powder and stir until just combined. Stir in the chocolate chips until evenly incorporated.

Spread half the batter into the prepared pan. Dollop and then gently swirl the remaining 2 tablespoons (32 g) of peanut butter into the batter. Add the remaining batter over the top; don't worry if it does not fully cover the peanut butter.

Arrange the pretzels over the top of the batter, gently pressing to adhere. Transfer to the oven and bake for 22 to 25 minutes, just until the blondies are set in the center. Remove the pan from the oven and sprinkle with the sea salt, if desired. Let the blondies cool completely before cutting into bars.

Cover and store leftover blondies in an airtight container at room temperature for 2 to 3 days.

pumpkin chocolate chip blondies

Come October, I'm always looking for ways to bake with pumpkin. Pumpkin and chocolate are one of those iconic fall pairings that never gets old. And I have to say that these moist, lightly spiced blondies are just about my favorite way to enjoy the two flavors together.

2⅓ cups (280 g) all-purpose flour

1 tbsp (6 g) pumpkin pie spice

1 tsp cinnamon

1 tsp baking soda

¾ tsp kosher salt

1 cup (230 g) unsalted butter, at room temperature

¾ cup (150 g) granulated sugar

¾ cup (165 g) dark brown sugar

1 large egg

2 tsp (10 ml) vanilla extract

15 oz (425 g) pure pumpkin puree

1 cup (175 g) dark chocolate chips

1 cup (180 g) white chocolate chips

¾ cup (85 g) pecans, roughly chopped, optional

Preheat the oven to 350°F (180°C). Grease a 9 x 13–inch (22 x 33–cm) pan with butter or nonstick cooking spray and then line the pan with parchment paper, leaving an overhang on all sides. Grease the parchment with butter or nonstick cooking spray and then set it aside.

In a medium bowl, whisk together the flour, pumpkin pie spice, cinnamon, baking soda and salt. Set it aside.

In the bowl of a stand mixer fitted with the paddle attachment, or in a large bowl using an electric hand mixer, cream the butter, granulated sugar and dark brown sugar on medium-high speed until smooth. Beat in the egg and vanilla until combined. Then beat in the pumpkin puree. If the mixture looks curdled, don't freak out!

Reduce the speed to low and mix in the dry ingredients until just combined. Fold in the dark and white chocolate chips and pecans, if using, with a rubber spatula.

Spread the batter evenly in the prepared pan. Bake for 35 to 40 minutes, until the edges begin to pull away from the sides of the pan and a tooth-pick inserted into the center comes out with just a few moist crumbs attached. Cool completely in the pan before cutting into bars.

Cover and store leftover blondies in an airtight container at room temperature for 2 to 3 days.

maple-glazed apple blondies

These blondies couldn't be more autumnal if they tried. I'm always so inspired to dive into fall baking; that crisp air just begs for something warm and cinnamony baking in the oven. These apple blondies are the answer. They come together in a snap and make your entire house smell incredible. And don't even get me started on that maple glaze! I recommend using an apple variety that's not only firm but also a little more on the tart side, such as Jonagolds, Granny Smiths or Cortlands.

BLONDIES

¾ cup (170 g) unsalted butter, melted

1 cup (200 g) granulated sugar

½ cup (110 g) light brown sugar

1 large egg + 1 egg yolk

1 tsp vanilla extract

¼ tsp salt

1 cup (120 g) all-purpose flour

2 tsp (4 g) ground cinnamon

½ tsp ground ginger

¼ tsp ground nutmeg

2 small apples, peeled, cored and chopped into small cubes (I used Granny Smith)

MAPLE GLAZE

2 tbsp (30 g) unsalted butter, melted

¼ cup (60 ml) pure maple syrup

½ cup (60 g) sifted powdered sugar

Salt, to taste

Preheat the oven to 350°F (180°C). Grease an 8 x 8–inch (20 x 20–cm) pan with butter or nonstick cooking spray and then line the pan with parchment paper, leaving an overhang on all sides. Grease the parchment with butter or nonstick cooking spray and then set it aside.

To make the blondies, in a medium bowl, whisk together the butter, granulated sugar and light brown sugar until smooth and combined. Add the egg, egg yolk, vanilla and salt, and whisk vigorously until smooth and combined. Fold in the flour, cinnamon, ginger and nutmeg until thoroughly mixed, then fold in the apples.

Spread the batter evenly into the prepared pan and bake for 25 to 30 minutes, or until the center is set and a toothpick inserted comes out clean. Be careful not to overbake! Allow the blondies to cool completely in the pan on a wire rack; while the blondies cool, make the glaze.

To make the maple glaze, in a medium bowl, whisk together the butter and maple syrup. Add the powdered sugar and stir until thoroughly combined. The glaze should be a pourable consistency but thick enough to coat a spoon. Add more powdered sugar if the glaze is too thin or more maple syrup if it's too thick. Add a pinch of salt if the glaze is too sweet. (I usually add anywhere between ⅛ to ¼ teaspoon of salt.) Drizzle the maple glaze on top of the cooled blondies before cutting into bars.

Cover and store leftover blondies in an airtight container at room temperature for 2 to 3 days.

cookies, but make them bars

Everyone has a favorite way to unwind after a long and tiring day of work. Some people head to the gym; others, to the bar; and still more, home to the living room couch. For me, after working all day, I go straight to the kitchen. I find baking relaxing. The familiar whiz of my electric stand mixer, the heat radiating from my tiny apartment oven and the smell of brown butter soothes my rattled nerves. When I get home from work, however, I usually want treats that require minimal effort, saving my more complicated bakes for weekends when I have more free time. That's where cookie bars come into play.

There's the traditional way of making a cookie: You make the dough, form little balls on a sheet pan and then bake them. At the end, you have a pile of cookies. However, you don't have to make them like that. As much as I love cookies, I know I can't be the only one who doesn't always want to take the time to shape them individually. That's why cookie bars like the ones you'll find in this chapter are perfect—all the dough gets dumped into a baking pan and out comes soft baked cookie bars!

One thing I love about cookie bars is how, much like brownies, there's no end to the creation of new and tasty flavor combinations. As a cookie lover, I have unearthed some real treasures since starting my blog a few years ago. One of my favorite cookies of all time is the Brown Butter Chocolate Chunk Cookie Bars (page 75), which I adapted from its traditional round counterpart that's available on my website. The easiest-to-make and most cherished are the gooey S'mores Bars (page 84). And if I had just one cookie to eat for the rest of time, it would be the perfectly sweet, yet tangy and over-the-top Frosted Sugar Cookie Bars (page 79).

TIPS & TECHNIQUES

- Keep your hands cold and wet. Just about every cookie bar recipe calls for pressing dough into the pan, and keeping your hands moist with a little bit of cold water prevents the dough from sticking. Be careful not to go overboard, you don't want to unintentionally add too much moisture to your dough.

- Measure your flour correctly. Adding too much flour to a recipe is never a good idea. Still, it can be seriously detrimental to cookie bars. The best and easiest way to measure flour is by using a scale. If you don't have one, then fluff your flour with a spoon, spoon it into your measuring cup and use a knife to level it off.

- Storage matters. Store cookie bars covered at room temperature for up to 3 days. Add an apple wedge, piece of bread or a tortilla on the top of the cookie bars to keep them softer for longer. You can also freeze them in an airtight container for up to 2 months. Defrost at room temperature and refresh in a 300°F (150°C) oven until warmed through, if desired. I don't recommend storing cookie bars in the fridge.

brown butter chocolate chunk cookie bars

These are a spin on the most popular cookie recipe on my website. The brown sugar helps to keep the cookie bars softer and chewier in the middle, yet still allows for crispy, delicious edges. And the brown butter . . . well, I'm a firm believer that brown butter makes just about any baked good better if you couldn't tell by now.

¾ cup (170 g) unsalted butter, cubed

1½ cups (330 g) dark brown sugar

½ cup (100 g) granulated sugar

1 tsp kosher salt

2 tsp (10 ml) vanilla extract

½ tsp espresso powder

3 large eggs + 1 egg yolk

2¼ tsp (12 g) baking powder

2¾ cups (330 g) all-purpose flour

8 oz (225 g) 70% cacao dark chocolate, chopped

Preheat the oven to 350°F (180°C). Grease a 9 x 13–inch (22 x 33–cm) pan with butter or nonstick cooking spray and then line the pan with parchment paper, leaving an overhang on all sides. Grease the parchment with butter or nonstick cooking spray and then set it aside.

Place the butter in a light-colored skillet. (A light-colored skillet will help you determine when the butter begins browning.) Melt the butter over medium heat, stirring constantly. Once melted, the butter will start to foam. Keep stirring. After 5 to 8 minutes, the butter will begin browning; you'll notice lightly browned specks begin to form at the bottom of the pan, and you'll start to smell a nutty aroma. Once browned, immediately remove from the heat, pour the butter into a large heatproof mixing bowl and set aside to cool slightly.

In the bowl of a stand mixer fitted with the paddle attachment, or using an electric hand mixer, cream together the dark brown sugar, granulated sugar, salt, vanilla, espresso powder and cooled brown butter until combined and fluffy, about 5 minutes.

Add the eggs and egg yolk and mix until incorporated. Add the baking powder and flour and mix until just combined. Fold the chopped chocolate into the dough.

Wet your hands slightly (to prevent sticking) and then press the dough into the prepared pan.

Bake for 28 to 32 minutes, or until the center is set and no longer jiggles when you shake the pan. Allow the bars to cool completely in the pan before removing and slicing.

Cover and store leftover bars in an airtight container at room temperature for 2 to 3 days.

TOTAL TIME: 1 hour
YIELD: 24 bars

magic cookie bars

Magic Cookie Bars (also known as Hello Dolly Bars or 7-Layer Bars) are some of the simplest, yet most decadent cookie bars you can bake. Eat one of these bad boys warm from the oven with a glass of cold milk and revel in the magic of how a few simple ingredients can be transformed into something so wickedly delicious.

½ cup (115 g) unsalted butter, melted

1½ cups (150 g) graham cracker crumbs, approximately 9 full-sheet graham crackers

1 cup (175 g) semisweet chocolate chips

1 cup (180 g) white chocolate chips

1 cup (110 g) chopped pecans, toasted

14 oz (420 ml) sweetened condensed milk

1 cup (84 g) unsweetened shredded coconut

½ cup (50 g) sweetened flaked coconut

Flaky sea salt, for garnish

Preheat the oven to 350°F (180°C). Grease a 9 x 13–inch (22 x 33–cm) pan with butter or nonstick cooking spray and then line the pan with parchment paper, leaving an overhang on all sides. Grease the parchment with butter or nonstick cooking spray and then set it aside.

In a small bowl, mix together the butter and graham cracker crumbs. Spread the crumbs evenly over the bottom of the prepared pan.

Evenly layer the top with the semisweet chocolate chips, white chocolate chips and chopped pecans. Pour the sweetened condensed milk evenly over the nuts. In an even layer, sprinkle the shredded and flaked coconut over the condensed milk. Gently press down the coconut.

Bake until the edges are golden brown, 23 to 25 minutes. Remove the bars from the oven, sprinkle with the flaky sea salt and allow them to cool completely in the pan before removing. You may cut the bars into any size you wish!

Cover and store leftover bars in an airtight container at room temperature for 2 to 3 days.

frosted sugar cookie bars

These Frosted Sugar Cookie Bars are soft, chewy and topped with creamy vanilla buttercream. The best part? It's an easy recipe to make, and then you just dump the dough into a pan and press flat. No dough balls, no cookie sheets going in and out of the oven every 10 minutes, just super simple steps!

COOKIE BARS

½ cup (115 g) unsalted butter, softened

1 cup (200 g) granulated sugar

1 large egg + 1 egg yolk

2 tbsp (35 g) sour cream

2 tsp (10 ml) vanilla extract

½ tsp almond extract

2 cups (240 g) all-purpose flour

1 tsp cornstarch

½ tsp baking soda

½ tsp baking powder

¼ tsp salt

VANILLA FROSTING (SEE NOTE)

¾ cup (170 g) unsalted butter, at room temperature

2¼ cups (270 g) powdered sugar

3 tbsp (45 ml) heavy cream

1 tsp vanilla extract

Salt, to taste

Food coloring, optional

NOTE: *If you don't want a super thick layer of frosting (as pictured), halve the frosting recipe.*

Preheat the oven to 350°F (180°C). Line an 8 x 8–inch (20 x 20–cm) pan with aluminum foil, making sure to leave enough overhang on the sides. Set it aside.

To make the cookie bars, in a large bowl using an electric hand mixer or in a stand mixer fitted with a paddle attachment, cream the softened butter for about 1 minute on medium speed. Get it nice and smooth, then add the granulated sugar and beat on medium speed until fluffy and light in color, 4 to 5 minutes. Beat in the egg, egg yolk, sour cream, vanilla extract and almond extract. Scrape down the sides as needed.

In a medium bowl, whisk together the flour, cornstarch, baking soda, baking powder and salt. With the mixer running on low speed, slowly add the dry ingredients to the wet ingredients in three different portions. The dough will be quite thick.

Once combined, wet your hands slightly (to prevent sticking) and then press the dough into the prepared pan.

Bake for 25 to 26 minutes, or until very lightly browned on top. You want the cookie bars to be extra soft, so be careful not to overbake them. Allow the bars to cool completely on a wire rack at room temperature before frosting. The center will sink slightly, which is normal.

To make the vanilla frosting, in a large bowl with an electric hand mixer or in a stand mixer fitted with a paddle attachment, beat the butter on medium speed until creamy, about 2 minutes. Add the powdered sugar, heavy cream and vanilla with the mixer running on low. Increase to high speed and beat for 3 full minutes. To check the consistency, tap the frosting with your index finger. If nothing sticks, it's still too thick. If your finger is coated in frosting and it's fairly sticky, it's too thin. You want it to be just sticky enough that some of your finger is covered, but not the whole thing. Add more powdered sugar if the frosting is too thin or more heavy cream if the frosting is too thick. Add a pinch of salt if the frosting is too sweet. (I usually add anywhere between ⅛ to ¼ teaspoon of salt.) Beat in the food coloring, if using.

Remove the cooled bars from the pan using the aluminum foil overhang on the sides. Frost the bars with a thick layer of frosting. Cut them into squares using a very sharp knife, wiping the knife clean with a paper towel between each cut. Cover and store leftover bars in an airtight container at room temperature for 2 to 3 days.

pb&j shortbread bars

Talk about nostalgia. These cookie bars take me back to brown-bag school lunches of peanut butter and jelly sandwiches. I'm a firm believer that there's no one "right" way to make a PB&J (at least when it comes to ingredients), so use whatever jam you prefer! A quick note on the peanut butter: I recommend using all-natural peanut butter (you know, the kind where the natural oils tend to separate) as you'll find it's easier to swirl into the jam.

1 cup (230 g) unsalted butter, at room temperature

½ cup (100 g) granulated sugar

1 tsp almond extract

½ tsp kosher salt

2 cups (240 g) all-purpose flour

1 cup (95 g) almond flour

½ cup (40 g) old-fashioned oats

¾ cup (240 g) of your favorite jam

6 tbsp (98 g) creamy peanut butter

Preheat the oven to 350°F (180°C). Grease an 8 x 8–inch (20 x 20–cm) pan with butter or nonstick cooking spray and then line the pan with parchment paper, leaving an overhang on all sides. Grease the parchment with butter or nonstick cooking spray and then set it aside.

In a stand mixer fitted with the paddle attachment, cream together the butter and sugar on medium-high speed until fluffy, 3 to 4 minutes. Add the almond extract and salt and mix briefly. Add the all-purpose flour and almond flour and mix until the dough is crumbly.

Take half of the dough and press it into the prepared pan in an even layer using your fingertips. Mix the old-fashioned oats into the dough still in the mixing bowl, then place it in the refrigerator.

Bake the shortbread dough for 25 minutes, then remove the pan from the oven. Spread the jam evenly over the top of the partially baked shortbread, then add the peanut butter by spooning on dollops. Swirl the two lightly with a spatula. Take out the reserved shortbread oat crumble and sprinkle it all over the top. Bake for an additional 20 to 25 minutes, until the bars are lightly browned on top. Let the bars cool completely, then cut into squares.

Cover and store leftover bars in an airtight container at room temperature for 2 to 3 days.

glazed gingerdoodle cookie bars

These Glazed Gingerdoodle Cookie Bars taste like a cross between a soft gingerbread cookie and a snickerdoodle with a cream cheese glaze that just sends them over the top. Add this to your baking list ASAP! You'll love the texture of the cookies, but more importantly, the molasses flavor with the cinnamon, ginger and cloves is irresistible!

COOKIE BARS

1 cup (120 g) all-purpose flour

½ tsp baking powder

¼ tsp baking soda

¼ tsp kosher salt

1 tsp cinnamon

6 tbsp (85 g) unsalted butter, melted

½ cup (110 g) light brown sugar

½ cup (100 g) granulated sugar

2 tbsp (30 ml) unsulphured molasses

2 tsp (10 ml) vanilla extract

1 tsp freshly grated ginger

1 large egg

CINNAMON-SUGAR TOPPING

2 tbsp (25 g) granulated sugar

¾ tsp ground cinnamon

CREAM CHEESE GLAZE

2 oz (60 g) cream cheese, softened

1 tbsp (15 g) unsalted butter, softened

½ tsp vanilla extract

½ cup (60 g) powdered sugar

Preheat the oven to 350°F (180°C). Grease an 8 x 8–inch (20 x 20–cm) pan with butter or nonstick cooking spray and then line the pan with parchment paper, leaving an overhang on all sides. Grease the parchment with butter or nonstick cooking spray and then set it aside.

To make the cookie bars, in a small bowl, whisk together the flour, baking powder, baking soda, salt and cinnamon.

In the bowl of a stand mixer fitted with the paddle attachment, or using an electric hand mixer, cream together the melted butter, light brown sugar and granulated sugar. Pour in the molasses, vanilla, ginger and egg and continue to mix.

Once the wet ingredients are mixed, slowly add in the dry ingredients and mix until just combined. Pour the batter into the prepared pan and spread out evenly.

To make the cinnamon-sugar topping, in a small bowl, whisk together the sugar and cinnamon. Sprinkle about half of the mixture on top of the cookie bars.

Bake the bars for 25 minutes, or until a toothpick comes out clean. Cool completely on a wire rack, then remove the bars. Sprinkle with the leftover cinnamon-sugar topping once baked, if desired.

To make the cream cheese glaze, in a microwave-safe bowl, combine the cream cheese, butter, vanilla and powdered sugar until well combined. Heat the glaze in the microwave in 10-second intervals until the glaze is a pourable consistency. Drizzle on top of the cookie bars and allow them to cool and set before slicing.

Cover and store leftover bars in an airtight container at room temperature for 2 to 3 days.

s'mores bars

Sometimes the best ideas come at the end of a long day when you're hungry and trying to figure out what to snack on. (Sometimes the worst ideas come at this time, too.) What you are about to witness is the marriage of a classic summer s'more (graham cracker, chocolate and marshmallow) with the form of a traditional cookie bar. The only thing you'll need to make from scratch is the graham cracker cookie dough. Hello, yes, GRAHAM CRACKER COOKIE DOUGH. What are you waiting for!?

1½ cups (180 g) all-purpose flour

1 cup (100 g) graham cracker crumbs, approximately 6 full-sheet graham crackers

1 tsp baking powder

¼ tsp kosher salt

1 cup (230 g) unsalted butter, softened

1¼ cups (275 g) dark brown sugar

2 large eggs

1½ tsp (8 ml) vanilla extract

2–3 cups (100–150 g) mini marshmallows

1 cup (175 g) milk chocolate chips or chopped milk chocolate bars

Graham cracker pieces, for garnish

Preheat the oven to 350°F (180°C). Grease a 9 x 13–inch (22 x 33–cm) pan with aluminum foil and grease the foil with butter or nonstick cooking spray. Set it aside.

In a large bowl, combine the flour, graham cracker crumbs, baking powder and salt. Set it aside.

In the bowl of a stand mixer fitted with the paddle attachment, or using an electric hand mixer, beat the butter and dark brown sugar until it's smooth and creamy, scraping the sides of the bowl as needed. Add the eggs and vanilla and beat to combine. Add the dry ingredients into the wet ingredients and beat until combined.

Add the dough to the prepared pan. Wet your hands slightly (to prevent sticking) and then press the dough into one smooth layer.

Bake for 25 minutes. A toothpick inserted into the center of the bars should come out clean. Remove from the oven and top with marshmallows and chocolate chips. Bake an additional 5 to 10 minutes, until the marshmallows are light golden brown. Sprinkle the top with crushed graham crackers, and then set the pan on a wire rack to cool completely.

Cover and store leftover bars in an airtight container at room temperature for 2 to 3 days.

oatmeal chocolate chip cookie bars

I realize that this is a potentially controversial statement, but I love oatmeal chocolate chip cookies possibly more than regular chocolate chip cookies. Let's be clear though—raisins have no place here! These cookie bars are so soft and chewy and, quite honestly, just perfect. Try them yourself and be amazed!

2½ cups (200 g) old-fashioned oats

2 cups (240 g) all-purpose flour

1 cup (220 g) dark brown sugar

½ cup (100 g) granulated sugar

1 tsp baking soda

1 tsp kosher salt

1 cup (240 ml) canola oil

2 large eggs

1 tbsp (15 ml) vanilla extract

1½ cups (260 g) semisweet chocolate chips, divided

Preheat the oven to 350°F (180°C). Grease a 9 x 13–inch (22 x 33–cm) pan with butter or nonstick cooking spray and then line the pan with parchment paper, leaving an overhang on all sides. Grease the parchment with butter or nonstick cooking spray and then set it aside.

In a large mixing bowl or the bowl of a stand mixer fitted with the paddle attachment, mix the oats, flour, dark brown sugar, granulated sugar, baking soda, salt, oil, eggs and vanilla. Beat until the dough is moist and all the ingredients are combined. (The dough will be crumbly.) Mix in 1 cup (175 g) of the chocolate chips.

Press the dough into the prepared pan and scatter the remaining chocolate chips on top. Transfer to the oven and bake for 18 to 20 minutes, or until the edges are set and the bars are golden. Let cool and then cut them into bars.

Cover and store leftover bars in an airtight container at room temperature for 2 to 3 days.

espresso carmelitas

Carmelitas are not your ordinary, run-of-the-mill treat. Instead, it's like a buttery oatmeal cookie that swallowed a caramel-and-nut-filled chocolate bar and then got bibitty-bobitty-booped by the dessert fairy godmother and received an extra dose of deliciousness. These carmelitas take it one step further by using an espresso caramel, but feel free to leave the espresso powder out if you're not a fan. The bars will still be delicious, I promise!

ESPRESSO CARAMEL

1 cup (200 g) granulated sugar

6 tbsp (85 g) unsalted butter

½ cup (120 ml) heavy cream

1½ tsp (3 g) espresso powder

1 tsp kosher salt

CARMELITAS

¾ cup (170 g) unsalted butter, melted

¾ cup (165 g) light brown sugar

2 tsp (10 ml) vanilla extract

1 cup (120 g) all-purpose flour

1 cup (80 g) old-fashioned oats

1 tsp baking soda

¼ tsp kosher salt

1 cup (175 g) semisweet chocolate chips

½ cup (55 g) pecans, chopped

1 batch espresso caramel

Preheat the oven to 350°F (180°C). Spray an 8 x 8–inch (20 x 20–cm) pan with nonstick cooking spray and line the pan with parchment paper with an overhang on two sides. Spray the parchment paper with nonstick cooking spray and set it aside.

To make the espresso caramel, in a medium saucepan over medium heat, add the granulated sugar, stirring with a high heat–resistant rubber spatula or wooden spoon. The sugar will form clumps and eventually melt into a thick, amber-colored liquid as you continue to stir. Be careful not to burn it! Once the sugar is completely dissolved, about 10 minutes, immediately add the butter and stir until melted, about 2 minutes. (Be careful with this step, because the caramel will bubble rapidly when the butter is added.) Very slowly drizzle in the heavy cream while stirring. Allow the mixture to boil for 30 to 45 seconds, then remove it from the heat. Stir in the espresso powder and salt and set it aside until needed.

To make the carmelitas, in a large bowl, combine the melted butter, light brown sugar, vanilla, flour, oats, baking soda and salt. Stir everything together with a fork. Press half of the mixture into the prepared pan. Bake for 10 minutes.

Remove the pan from the oven and sprinkle the top evenly with the chocolate chips and pecans, and then with the espresso caramel. Crumble the remaining oat mixture over the caramel. Return the pan to the oven and continue to bake for 18 to 20 minutes, just until the edges are lightly browned. Remove from the oven. Cool in the pan on a wire rack at least 3 hours before removing and cutting into bars.

Cover and store leftover bars in an airtight container at room temperature for 2 to 3 days.

rich, velvety cheesecake bars

When I was younger, the idea of a dessert made of cheese repulsed me. The very phrase was an injustice and a perfect representation of how taste buds go awry as people age. Grown-ups ate cottage cheese, for crying out loud. I was told sweet potatoes tasted like candy. Really, how could their tastes be trusted? To me, cakes were to be cake-like: yellow, layered and frosted. They weren't supposed to be white, and they weren't supposed to have a crust made of graham crackers.

When offered, I refused to try even the smallest bite. That is, until college. Cheesecake was literally always available in the dining halls. I couldn't understand it, frankly. Who wanted it there? Who was eating it? That question came up one evening at dinner, and my friends couldn't believe I'd never tried it. After enduring the peer pressure for the rest of that night's meal, I figured why not, right? And so, at the age of 18, I had my first cheesecake. It was, as you probably have known for years, sweet, light and creamy. Absolutely delicious. "It's not bad, I guess," I mumbled, refusing to give my friends the satisfaction of being right. Meanwhile, I grieved over cheesecake-eating opportunities I'd lost to stubbornness and ignorance.

Nowadays, a slice of luxuriously rich New York–style cheesecake has become one of my favorite guilty pleasures, especially since moving to the city. If it's on the menu, you can probably bet that I'm going to order it. But despite this now-existing love of cheesecake, I rarely make cheesecake at home, because it can be a bit fussy. Cheesecake bars, however, are a completely different story. You get all the great flavor of cheesecake without the fuss of making a big cheesecake. Total game-changer. If you're new to baking cheesecakes, cheesecake bars are the perfect place to start; if you're an experienced baker, you'll still appreciate them for their ease.

TIPS & TECHNIQUES

- Use room-temperature cream cheese. Just about every cheesecake bar recipe calls for "softened" cream cheese—and that's no accident. Softened cream cheese is creamier when mixed, and it combines better with the other ingredients in the recipe. If the cream cheese is too cold, your mixture will be lumpy, and so will your finished cheesecake.

- If you don't have time to wait for the cream cheese to soften at room temperature, here's an alternative: Put your cream cheese bricks (still in their foil wrapping) in a sealed ziplock bag and submerge them in warm water for approximately 10 to 15 minutes.

- Don't overmix your batter. It's all about balance. You want to mix the cream cheese enough to remove any lumps, but not so much that you incorporate too much air, which can cause the cheesecake to rise too rapidly in the oven, then fall and crack while cooling.

- Since eggs are the ingredient that really holds the air, a good guideline is to mix thoroughly at first, when you're combining cream cheese and sugar, but beat more gently once the eggs are incorporated. Also, scrape, scrape and scrape again while mixing to make sure no lumps are clinging to the sides of the bowl.

- Let the bars cool gradually. Cheesecake bars pretty much require being made a day in advance. After careful baking and slow cooling, the cheesecake will still need to chill in the fridge and finish setting before being sliced into bars.

- It's essential to let the cheesecake come to room temperature completely before placing in the fridge to chill. If a warm cheesecake is rushed straight into the refrigerator, the cake will contract dramatically, and a sticky condensation layer will form on top, affecting the texture.

vanilla chai cheesecake bars

While traditional, authentic cheesecakes have their place, I sometimes (read: usually) don't want to mess with a water bath, the risk of a cracked cheesecake top, extra-long baking time and meticulous instructions. If you are looking for excellent cheesecake taste without most of the fuss, this recipe fits the bill. Baked with just a few simple ingredients, these cheesecake bars taste like your favorite chai latte. Featuring flavorful swirls of chai-infused cream cheese filling, each bite offers richly aromatic, spiced flavor set against a cool and creamy vanilla cheesecake backdrop. They're such a simple dessert to make, but undeniably impressive. And if you're worried about the chai being too intense, don't be—it's just the right amount of spice, warmth and sweetness, I promise!

CRUST

1¼ cups (125 g) graham cracker crumbs, approximately 8 full-sheet graham crackers

⅓ cup (75 g) dark brown sugar

½ tsp ground cinnamon

¼ tsp kosher salt

5 tbsp (75 g) unsalted butter, melted

CHEESECAKE

16 oz (450 g) cream cheese, softened

1 cup (200 g) granulated sugar

¼ cup (60 ml) heavy cream, at room temperature

3 large eggs, at room temperature

2 tsp (10 g) vanilla bean paste

1 tsp lemon juice

½ tsp ground cinnamon

½ tsp ground ginger

¼ tsp ground cardamom

¼ tsp allspice

Pinch of black pepper

Preheat the oven to 375°F (190°C). Grease an 8 x 8–inch (20 x 20–cm) pan with butter or nonstick cooking spray and then line the pan with parchment paper, leaving an overhang on all sides. Grease the parchment with butter or nonstick cooking spray and then set it aside.

To make the crust, in a medium bowl, whisk together the graham cracker crumbs, dark brown sugar, cinnamon and salt. Add the melted butter and stir until well combined. Press the mixture firmly into the bottom of the prepared pan. Place the pan into the freezer for at least 15 minutes before baking.

Bake the crust for 10 minutes, until the edges are light golden brown. Remove the crust from the oven, set it aside to cool slightly while you make the cheesecake batter and reduce the oven temperature to 325°F (160°C).

To make the cheesecake, in the bowl of a stand mixer fitted with the paddle attachment, beat the cream cheese and granulated sugar together on medium-low speed until smooth. Add the heavy cream and then the eggs, one at a time, beating on low speed between each addition.

Add the vanilla bean paste, lemon juice, cinnamon, ginger, cardamom, allspice and black pepper and beat until evenly incorporated. Be careful not to overmix!

Pour the batter onto the slightly cooled crust and firmly tap the pan on a hard surface to release any air bubbles.

Check to make sure your oven has cooled to 325°F (160°C), then bake for 35 to 40 minutes, until the filling is set but still a little jiggly in the center. An instant-read thermometer, inserted into the filling about 1 inch (2.5 cm) in from the edge, should read between 180 and 190°F (82 and 87°C). The cheesecake will continue to cook as it cools.

(continued)

vanilla chai cheesecake bars (continued)

Let the bars cool at room temperature for 2 hours, and then refrigerate until cold, at least 3 hours but preferably overnight.

Use the parchment paper overhang to lift the cheesecake out of the pan and onto a cutting board. Cut into squares, wiping the knife clean with a warm, damp cloth between slices. Refrigerate until ready to serve.

Cover and store leftover bars in an airtight container in the refrigerator for 5 to 7 days.

no-bake blueberry-lavender swirl cheesecake bars

Of all the cheesecakes I created for this book, this was my favorite one to make, and I never got sick of eating it. The best part, by far, is that it's a no-bake recipe that comes together quickly. The hardest part is waiting for it to chill before you dig in.

This no-bake base recipe comes from my friend Erin Clarkson. Erin is a food blogger, too, and we spend an embarrassing amount of time texting each other about baking—usually brainstorming ideas and occasionally collaborating on recipes. When I told her I had been looking for the perfect no-bake cheesecake recipe, she directed me toward one of her recipes. I've taken her base and made a few tweaks to it, but it's otherwise PERFECT. Try for yourself and see!

BLUEBERRY COULIS SWIRL (SEE NOTE)

8 oz (225 g) fresh blueberries

¼ cup (50 g) granulated sugar, plus more to taste

2 tbsp (30 ml) lemon juice

1 tsp culinary-grade lavender

GRAHAM CRACKER CRUST

3 cups (300 g) graham cracker crumbs, approximately 18 full-sheet graham crackers

¼ cup (55 g) light brown sugar

¼ cup (55 g) dark brown sugar

¼ tsp kosher salt

10 tbsp (150 g) unsalted butter, melted

Line a 9 x 13–inch (22 x 33–cm) pan with parchment paper, extending the parchment paper over the sides to form a sling.

To make the blueberry coulis swirl, in a medium saucepan over medium heat, cook the blueberries, sugar and lemon juice, stirring often and occasionally mashing the berries against the side of the pan. After 5 to 7 minutes, the berries will start releasing their juices. Add the lavender and allow it to steep until the berries are soft, about 10 minutes. Transfer the mixture to a blender or food processor (be careful as it will be hot), and blend until smooth.

Clean the saucepan and return it to the stove. Strain the blended berry mixture into the pan, then bring it to a boil and cook over medium heat, constantly stirring, for 2 to 3 minutes or until it's slightly thickened. Transfer the coulis to a container and allow it to cool completely, 30 minutes to an hour.

To make the graham cracker crust, in the bowl of a food processor, pulse the graham crackers, light brown sugar, dark brown sugar and salt until the crackers resemble fine crumbs. Transfer the mixture to a medium bowl. Add the melted butter and mix to combine; it should have the consistency of wet sand. Pour the crust into the prepared pan and pat it down until smooth using the bottom of a flat glass or a measuring cup, ensuring that it is an even thickness. Place the crust in the freezer while you prepare the filling.

(continued)

no-bake blueberry–lavender swirl cheesecake bars (continued)

CHEESECAKE FILLING

2 tsp (8 g) powdered gelatin

1¾ cups (420 ml) heavy cream, divided

16 oz (450 g) cream cheese, softened

¾ cup (150 g) granulated sugar

1 tsp vanilla bean paste

½ tsp kosher salt

To make the cheesecake filling, in a small saucepan over low heat, dissolve the gelatin in ½ cup (120 ml) of heavy cream. Set it aside.

In the bowl of a stand mixer fitted with the whisk attachment, or using an electric hand mixer, whip the remaining 1¼ cups (300 ml) of heavy cream until medium peaks form. Transfer it into a bowl and set aside.

In the same bowl used to whip the heavy cream (there's no need to wash it), whip the cream cheese and granulated sugar in the mixer until smooth. Add the vanilla bean paste and salt and beat to incorporate, then add the gelatin and cream mixture and mix well.

Remove the bowl from the mixer and, using a spatula, gently fold the whipped cream into the cream cheese mixture. Spoon the filling over the prepared base, tapping to remove any bubbles, then spread with an offset spatula.

Evenly distribute 3 to 4 tablespoons (45 to 60 ml) of the cooled coulis mixture over the surface of the filling, and gently mix it into the top section of the filling using a spoon, before smoothing again with an offset spatula. Lightly drizzle a little more of the coulis mixture (use less than you think you will need) over the top of the cheesecake, then drag a skewer through the drizzled coulis to make a marbled effect. Add more coulis and marble more as desired.

Refrigerate the cheesecake for at least 3 hours or until set. Using the parchment paper as a sling, remove the cheesecake from the pan. Cut into squares using a knife that has been run through hot water and then dried before cutting. Cover and store leftover bars in an airtight container in the refrigerator for 5 to 7 days.

NOTE: *The leftover blueberry coulis will keep for a week if stored in an airtight container in the fridge.*

margarita cheesecake bars

Anyone who knows me knows that my all-time favorite cocktail is a margarita. So when I was working on this recipe, it was important to me that I nailed it. For this cheesecake, the usual cream cheese, heavy cream, eggs and sugar are flavored with lime juice, lime zest, triple sec and tequila. Enough for a little zip! Plus, if you didn't realize it, alcohol is a flavor enhancer just like salt. So, all the additions play a role in making one sweet, tangy and limey dessert.

CRUST

1¼ cups (125 g) graham cracker crumbs, approximately 8 full-sheet graham crackers

⅓ cup (75 g) light brown sugar

½ tsp ground cinnamon

Pinch of kosher salt

5 tbsp (75 g) unsalted butter, melted

FILLING

16 oz (450 g) cream cheese, softened

1 cup (200 g) granulated sugar

¼ cup (60 ml) heavy cream, at room temperature

3 large eggs, at room temperature

2 tbsp (30 ml) lime juice

1½ tbsp (23 ml) tequila

1 tsp triple sec

Zest of 1 lime

Preheat the oven to 375°F (190°C). Line an 8 x 8–inch (20 x 20–cm) pan with parchment paper, extending the parchment paper over the sides to form a sling.

To make the crust, in a large bowl, add the graham cracker crumbs, light brown sugar, cinnamon and salt. Stir the butter in with a fork and then press the mixture into the bottom of the prepared pan.

Bake for 8 to 10 minutes, until the crust is firm and has set. Remove from the oven and set it aside to cool.

To make the filling, in the bowl of a stand mixer fitted with the paddle attachment, beat the cream cheese and sugar together until well combined.

Add the heavy cream, eggs, lime juice, tequila, triple sec and lime zest. Continue beating until well combined.

Pour the filling into the crust and bake for 35 to 40 minutes, until the filling is set. It will be a little jiggly in the center, but firm, and will continue to cook and set as it cools.

Remove the pan from the oven and set it aside for 30 to 45 minutes to cool. Then refrigerate for at least 2 hours, preferably overnight, before serving.

Cover and store leftover bars in an airtight container in the refrigerator for 5 to 7 days.

no–bake oreo® cheesecake bites

These creamy No-Bake Oreo® Cheesecake Bites are the easiest dessert to make, ever, period. You don't need to turn on any stove or oven. There's a little bit of beating and creaming, but you really can't go wrong. The most challenging part of making this recipe is resisting the temptation to snack on all of the cookies. If you can do that, you're golden!

CRUST

30 cream-filled chocolate sandwich cookies (I like Oreos)

6 tbsp (85 g) unsalted butter, melted

FILLING

1 cup (240 ml) heavy whipping cream

¾ cup (150 g) granulated sugar, divided

1 tsp vanilla bean paste

16 oz (450 g) cream cheese, softened

Grease an 8 x 8–inch (20 x 20–cm) pan with butter or nonstick cooking spray and then line the pan with parchment paper, leaving an overhang on all sides. Grease the parchment with butter or nonstick cooking spray and then set it aside.

To make the crust, in a food processor, finely grind the cookies, reserving 1 cup (145 g) to mix with the filling. Add the rest to a medium mixing bowl. Add the melted butter to the ground cookies in the mixing bowl and use a fork to stir them together. Pour the crumbs into the prepared pan and press them firmly and evenly using the bottom of a flat glass or measuring cup. Place the pan in the freezer to firm up while you prepare the filling.

To make the filling, in the bowl of a stand mixer fitted with the whisk attachment, or using an electric hand mixer, whip the heavy cream, ¼ cup (50 g) of sugar and the vanilla bean paste until medium peaks form. Transfer into a bowl and set aside.

In the same mixing bowl you whipped the heavy cream in (no need to wash), whip the cream cheese and remaining ½ cup (100 g) of sugar in the mixer until smooth.

Remove the bowl from the mixer and, using a spatula, gently fold the whipped cream and reserved cookie crumbs into the cream cheese mixture. Spoon the filling over the prepared base, tapping to remove any bubbles, and then spread it evenly with an offset spatula.

Refrigerate the cheesecake for at least 3 hours or until set. Using the parchment paper as a sling, remove the cheesecake from the pan. Cut into squares using a knife that has been run through hot water and then dried before cutting.

Cover and store leftover bars in an airtight container in the refrigerator for 5 to 7 days.

toffee cheesecake bars

I have a love-hate relationship with toffee; I love toffee for its crunch, its flavor and its versatility, but I hate it because it always gets stuck in my teeth. First-world problems, am I right? I'm able to look past the small amount of disdain I have for toffee, however, when it comes to these cheesecake bars. These melt-in-your-mouth treats come together in no time and are absolutely delicious; everyone will want seconds. You've been warned!

CRUST

1 cup (120 g) all-purpose flour

¾ cup (90 g) powdered sugar

⅓ cup (25 g) unsweetened natural or Dutch-process cocoa powder

⅛ tsp baking soda

½ cup (115 g) unsalted butter, cold and cubed

FILLING

8 oz (225 g) cream cheese, softened

14 oz (420 ml) sweetened condensed milk

2 large eggs

1 tsp vanilla bean paste

1⅓ cups (225 g) milk chocolate toffee bits, divided

Preheat the oven to 350°F (180°C). Line a 9 x 13–inch (22 x 33–cm) pan with parchment paper and set it aside.

To make the crust, in the bowl of a food processor, combine the flour, powdered sugar, cocoa powder and baking soda. Add the cubed butter and process until the mixture resembles coarse crumbs. Press the mixture into the bottom of the prepared pan and bake for 13 to 15 minutes. The crust is done when it is slightly puffed.

To make the filling, in the bowl of a stand mixer fitted with the paddle attachment, or in a large bowl using an electric hand mixer, beat the cream cheese until it's fluffy. Add the sweetened condensed milk, eggs and vanilla bean paste and beat until smooth. Stir in ¾ cup (126 g) of the toffee bits. Pour the mixture over the crust. Bake for 18 to 22 minutes or until the center is almost set.

Cool on a wire rack for 15 minutes. Sprinkle with the remaining toffee bits, then cool completely. Cover and refrigerate for at least 3 hours or overnight before removing the bars from the pan and slicing.

Cover and store leftover bars in an airtight container in the refrigerator for 5 to 7 days.

chocolate-covered strawberry cheesecake bites

Dipping things in chocolate is all the rage. It's like the trend that never goes out of style, because you're always bound to end up with something amazing. Like these adorable little cubes that combine chocolate, strawberries and cheesecake into a mouthwatering, bite-size treat. Make these your next weekend baking project. You won't regret it!

STRAWBERRY PUREE

8 oz (225 g) chopped strawberries

¼ cup (50 g) granulated sugar

2 tbsp (30 ml) lemon juice

GRAHAM CRACKER CRUST

1½ cups (150 g) graham cracker crumbs, approximately 9 full-sheet graham crackers

¼ cup (50 g) granulated sugar

½ tsp kosher salt

½ cup (115 g) unsalted butter, melted

CHEESECAKE FILLING

¾ cup (180 ml) heavy cream

8 oz (225 g) cream cheese, softened

½ cup (100 g) granulated sugar

½ tsp vanilla bean paste

¼ tsp kosher salt

1 batch strawberry puree

Line an 8 x 8–inch (20 x 20–cm) pan with parchment paper, extending the parchment paper over the sides to form a sling. Cover a baking sheet in parchment paper.

To make the strawberry puree, in a medium saucepan over medium heat, place the strawberries, granulated sugar and lemon juice. Cook, stirring often and occasionally mashing the berries against the side of the pan, for 8 to 10 minutes. Once the berries have released most of their juices, transfer to a blender or food processor (be careful as it will be hot) and blend until smooth.

Strain the blended strawberry mixture back into the pan, then bring it to a boil and cook over medium heat, constantly stirring, for 2 to 3 minutes or until slightly thickened and reduced. Transfer to a heatproof bowl and allow to cool completely.

To make the graham cracker crust, in the bowl of a food processor, add the graham crackers, sugar and salt. Pulse until the crackers resemble fine crumbs. Add the melted butter and mix to combine; it should have the consistency of wet sand. Pour the crust into the prepared pan and press down firmly until smooth using the bottom of a flat glass or a measuring cup, ensuring that it is an even thickness. Place the crust in the freezer while you prepare the filling.

To make the cheesecake filling, in the bowl of a stand mixer fitted with the whisk attachment, or using an electric hand mixer, whip the heavy cream until stiff peaks form. Transfer into a bowl and set aside.

In the same mixing bowl you used to whip the heavy cream (no need to wash it), whip the cream cheese and granulated sugar until smooth. Add the vanilla bean paste, salt and cooled strawberry puree and beat to incorporate.

Remove the bowl from the mixer and, using a spatula, gently fold the whipped cream into the cream cheese mixture. Spoon the filling over the prepared base, tapping to remove any bubbles, then spread it with an offset spatula. Place the pan in the freezer to chill for 1 hour.

(continued)

chocolate-covered strawberry cheesecake bites (continued)

CHOCOLATE COATING

16 oz (450 g) semisweet chocolate

¼ cup (58 g) unsalted butter

Once frozen, lift the cheesecake out of the pan and gently peel away the parchment paper. Using a sharp knife, cut the cheesecake into 36 bite-size squares. If the squares become too soft, freeze until chilled again.

To make the chocolate coating, place the chocolate and butter in a microwave-safe bowl and heat for 1 to 2 minutes in the microwave, stirring every 30 seconds until melted and smooth. Dip the cheesecake squares, one at a time, into the melted chocolate. Let the excess chocolate drip off and then place the bites on the parchment-covered baking sheet. Refrigerate the bites until the chocolate is set.

Cover and store leftover bites in an airtight container in the refrigerator for 5 to 7 days.

easy as pie

I'm going to let you in on a little secret: I love pies and tarts, but I hate making pie dough with a passion. That was the driving inspiration behind half of the recipes in this chapter, actually. Now I know some of you are thinking, "But pie dough is so easy!" or "Homemade is so much better than store-bought!" or even "You're a baker and food blogger, how could you?!" I hear you. I even agree with you, but I've come to the realization that just because I CAN make something from scratch doesn't mean I HAVE to. There are some shortcuts in baking that I'm OK with, and store-bought pie or pastry dough is often one of them. The recipes in this chapter eliminate the need for pie dough altogether, however, by either opting for a buttery graham cracker or shortbread crust.

This chapter includes some of my favorite ways to incorporate fruit into baked goods. After all, everyone knows a dessert with fruit in it basically makes it a healthy treat! That's my thought process, at least. If I had to pick a recipe to eat over and over and over again, it would be the Apple Crisp Bars (page 115). The brown butter shortbread crust with that perfectly spiced apple filling?! DROOL. And if you're looking to get away with eating dessert for breakfast, I encourage you to try the Strawberry Oatmeal Bars (page 119). I mean, oatmeal is a breakfast food, right?! And the strawberries can totally be swapped out for any other berry, making them super versatile. Of course, non-fruit pies need their love too. Gooey Pecan Pie Bars (page 124) and Pumpkin Pie Crumb Bars (page 123) are fun twists on everyone's favorite Thanksgiving pies and are my go-to desserts for fall-themed get-togethers.

TIPS & TECHNIQUES

- Choose fresh over frozen. When it comes to flavor, fresh fruit is always better than frozen. Often, when baking with frozen fruit, the fruit lacks in flavor and increases the water content in a recipe—which results in a liquid-y or mushy filling and/or crust. If frozen is your only option, be sure to thaw and drain the fruit completely before adding it to the mixing bowl!

- Keep it clean. Ensure your fruit is well washed and dried. It's important to clean your fresh fruit to ensure no dirt or pesticides are being added to the recipe.

- Pat freshly cut fruit dry. Too much fruit juice can sometimes really throw off a recipe, making your bar oddly moist and sticky. So whenever you're working with freshly cut fruit, be sure to lightly pat it dry.

apple crisp bars

I'm all about the warm and cozy taste and texture of apple pie, but I have fun baking those flavors into other desserts, like these Apple Crisp Bars. They're sturdy enough that they can be picked up and eaten with your hands, no fork required. But, if you want to throw a piece on a plate and add a scoop of vanilla ice cream, I'm definitely not judging you!

SHORTBREAD CRUST

1 cup (230 g) unsalted butter, cubed

½ cup (110 g) dark brown sugar

½ cup (100 g) granulated sugar

½ tsp kosher salt

2 cups (240 g) all-purpose flour

FILLING

6 large apples, peeled and thinly sliced (I like to use Honeycrisp, Granny Smith, Jonagold, Braeburn or Pink Lady)

¼ cup (50 g) granulated sugar

2 tsp (4 g) ground cinnamon

½ tsp ground nutmeg

¼ tsp ground cloves

¼ cup (30 g) all-purpose flour

CRUMBLE

1 cup (80 g) old-fashioned oats

½ cup (110 g) dark brown sugar

½ tsp ground cinnamon

½ cup (60 g) all-purpose flour

½ cup (115 g) unsalted butter, cold and cubed

Preheat the oven to 325°F (160°C). Line a 9 x 13–inch (22 x 33–cm) pan with aluminum foil or parchment paper, leaving an overhang on all sides. Set the pan aside.

To make the shortbread crust, place the butter in a light-colored skillet. (The light-colored skillet will help you determine when the butter begins browning.) Melt the butter over medium heat, stirring constantly. Once melted, the butter will start to foam. Keep stirring. After 5 to 8 minutes, the butter will begin browning; you'll notice lightly browned specks begin to form at the bottom of the pan, and you'll start to smell a nutty aroma. Once browned, immediately remove from the heat, pour into a large, heatproof mixing bowl and set aside to cool slightly.

In a medium bowl, stir together the cooled brown butter, dark brown sugar, granulated sugar and salt. Add the flour and stir until everything is combined. Press the mixture evenly into the prepared pan and bake for 15 to 17 minutes while you prepare the apple filling and crumble. The crust should be a light golden brown and slightly puffed. Once you remove the crust from the oven, turn the oven up to 350°F (180°C).

To make the filling, in a large bowl, combine the sliced apples, granulated sugar, cinnamon, nutmeg and cloves. Once the apples are evenly coated, let the mixture sit and macerate for 30 minutes, stirring occasionally. After 30 minutes, add the flour and stir until evenly combined.

To make the crumble, in a medium bowl, whisk together the oats, dark brown sugar, cinnamon and flour. Cut in the chilled butter with a pastry blender or two forks until the mixture resembles coarse crumbs. Set it aside.

Evenly layer the apples on top of the warm crust and press them down slightly so they're tightly packed. Sprinkle the apple layer with the crumble and bake for 30 to 35 minutes or until the crumble is golden brown.

Remove the pan from the oven and allow the bars to cool for at least 20 minutes at room temperature, then chill in the refrigerator for at least 2 hours or overnight.

Lift the parchment out of the pan using the overhang on the sides and slice. These apple crisp bars can be enjoyed cold, warm or at room temperature. Cover and store leftover bars in an airtight container in the refrigerator for 4 to 5 days.

brûléed meyer lemon bars

Packed with the juice of four Meyer lemons and a bit of zest, these creamy, tangy lemon bars are bursting with fresh lemon flavor. I think my favorite part of these Brûléed Meyer Lemon Bars is that they are so quick and easy to make. Instead of making a proper curd, these have a simple mix poured over the crust that bakes up and gets curd-like, which means you are all ready to go the moment the crust is ready. Plus, the brûléed top is just the icing (or caramel) on top! If you don't have a kitchen torch, or if you just prefer it, dust with powdered sugar for a more traditional finish.

SHORTBREAD CRUST

¼ cup (50 g) granulated sugar

¼ cup (55 g) light brown sugar

1¼ cups (150 g) all-purpose flour

¼ tsp kosher salt

½ cup (115 g) unsalted butter, melted

½ tsp vanilla extract

FILLING

4 large eggs

¾ cup (150 g) granulated sugar

⅓ cup (40 g) all-purpose flour

⅔ cup (160 ml) Meyer lemon juice, approximately 4 lemons

Zest of 2 Meyer lemons

BRÛLÉED TOPPING

Granulated sugar, for topping

Preheat the oven to 350°F (180°C). Grease an 8 x 8–inch (20 x 20–cm) pan with butter or nonstick cooking spray and then line the pan with parchment paper, leaving an overhang on all sides. Grease the parchment with butter or nonstick cooking spray and then set it aside.

To make the shortbread crust, in a medium bowl, whisk together the granulated sugar, light brown sugar, flour and salt. Slowly add the melted butter and vanilla to the flour mixture, stirring with a fork until combined. Press the mixture into the bottom of the prepared pan.

Bake for 15 minutes, until puffed and lightly golden.

To make the filling, in a large bowl, whisk together the eggs and granulated sugar until well combined and thick. Add the flour, lemon juice and lemon zest; whisk until combined, then pour it onto the warm crust.

Bake for 25 minutes, until the center is just set. Remove the bars from the oven and allow them to cool completely in the pan.

Once cool, run a knife around the edges of the pan to remove the lemon bars and then slice them into squares.

To make the brûléed topping, just before serving, generously sprinkle each lemon bar square with granulated sugar. Use a kitchen torch to caramelize the sugar until it is amber or golden brown.

Allow the bars to rest a few minutes so the sugar can harden and crisp before serving.

Cover and store leftover bars in an airtight container in the refrigerator for 4 to 5 days.

strawberry oatmeal bars

These bars are perfect for breakfast, a snack or dinner! The oats give the bars a deliciously chewy texture, and the natural sweetness of the strawberries lets you use much less sugar than you'd typically use in a dessert bar recipe. Add just a touch of cinnamon and these strawberry bars are almost impossible to resist!

CRUST AND CRUMBLE

1 cup (80 g) old-fashioned rolled oats

¾ cup (90 g) all-purpose flour

½ cup (110 g) dark brown sugar

½ tsp ground cinnamon

¼ tsp kosher salt

6 tbsp (85 g) unsalted butter, melted

FILLING

2 cups (350 g) diced, fresh strawberries

2 tbsp (25 g) granulated sugar

1 tsp cornstarch

1 tsp lemon juice

GLAZE

½ cup (60 g) powdered sugar

½ tsp vanilla bean paste

1 tbsp (15 ml) milk

Preheat the oven to 375°F (190°C). Line an 8 x 8–inch (20 x 20–cm) pan with parchment paper, leaving an overhang of parchment paper on all sides. Set it aside.

To make the crust and crumble, in a medium bowl, stir the oats, flour, dark brown sugar, cinnamon and salt together until combined. Stir the melted butter into the oatmeal mixture until it forms clumps. Set aside approximately ½ cup (56 g) of the crumble mixture. Press the remaining crumble mixture into an even layer in the bottom of the prepared pan.

To make the filling, in a small bowl, toss the strawberries, sugar, cornstarch and lemon juice together, then evenly spread the mixture over the crust. Sprinkle the reserved crumble over the fruit filling. The crumble won't completely cover the fruit.

Bake the bars for 35 to 45 minutes, or until the topping is light golden brown. Cool the bars in the pan until they reach room temperature.

To make the glaze, in a small bowl, whisk together the powdered sugar, vanilla bean paste and milk until combined. Drizzle the glaze over the cooled bars before cutting into squares.

Cover and store leftover bars in an airtight container in the refrigerator for 4 to 5 days.

key lime pie bars

These bars are everything you love about traditional Key lime pie, with a delicious twist! The cream cheese helps to thicken the bars a bit and give them a little more creaminess and tang. Keep in mind that this recipe calls for Key limes, which are different from regular limes in both flavor and size. Key limes are about the size of ping-pong balls and juicing them can take quite a long time, but I promise it's worth it!

CRUST

1½ cups (150 g) graham cracker crumbs, approximately 9 full-sheet graham crackers

⅓ cup (75 g) dark brown sugar

¼ tsp kosher salt

5 tbsp (75 g) unsalted butter, melted

KEY LIME PIE FILLING

6 oz (170 g) cream cheese, at room temperature

14 oz (420 ml) sweetened condensed milk

4 egg yolks

1 tbsp (9 g) lime zest

½ cup (120 ml) Key lime juice

½ tsp vanilla extract

Lime wedges, for garnish, optional

Preheat the oven to 350°F (180°C). Line an 8 x 8–inch (20 x 20–cm) pan with aluminum foil or parchment paper, leaving an overhang on all sides. Set it aside.

To make the crust, in a medium mixing bowl, combine the graham cracker crumbs, dark brown sugar, salt and butter, and mix to combine. Press the crumbs firmly and evenly into the bottom of the prepared pan.

Bake for 10 to 12 minutes, until the edges are light golden brown.

To make the Key lime pie filling, in a large mixing bowl with a hand mixer, beat the cream cheese until smooth and creamy. Add the sweetened condensed milk and mix until combined. Then add the egg yolks one at a time, mixing well after each addition, followed by the lime zest, lime juice and vanilla. Mix until it's combined.

Pour the filling over the hot, baked crust. Return the pan to the oven and bake for 18 to 22 minutes, or until set. The top should not brown.

Remove the pan from the oven and allow the bars to cool at room temperature before chilling them in the refrigerator for 2 to 4 hours. Garnish with lime wedges, if using.

Cover and store leftover bars in an airtight container in the refrigerator for 4 to 5 days.

pumpkin pie crumb bars

These Pumpkin Pie Crumb Bars are a cross between pumpkin pie and coffee cake with a crumb topping. The creamy pumpkin filling pairs perfectly with the buttery crust and topping. They make for a perfect no-fuss and low-key Thanksgiving dessert or just as a treat with a cup of coffee. Make sure you use pumpkin pie mix and NOT pumpkin puree or canned pumpkin; otherwise, your bars just won't set properly.

CRUST AND TOPPING

1 cup (220 g) dark brown sugar

3 cups (360 g) all-purpose flour

1 tsp baking soda

1 tsp baking powder

2 tsp (4 g) ground cinnamon

½ tsp ground cloves

½ tsp kosher salt

1 cup (230 g) unsalted butter, melted

FILLING

30 oz (850 g) canned pumpkin pie mix

2 large eggs

1½ tsp (8 ml) vanilla extract

Preheat the oven to 350°F (180°C). Grease a 9 x 13–inch (22 x 33–cm) pan with butter or nonstick cooking spray and then line the pan with parchment paper, leaving an overhang on all sides. Grease the parchment with butter or nonstick cooking spray and then set it aside.

To make the crust and topping, in a large bowl, whisk together the dark brown sugar, flour, baking soda, baking powder, cinnamon, cloves and salt until combined. Stir in the melted butter until a crumbly dough forms. Set aside approximately 1½ cups (185 g) of the mixture for the topping. Press the remaining dough into an even layer in the bottom of the prepared pan. Set it aside.

To make the filling, use an electric hand mixer or stand mixer fitted with a whisk attachment to whisk the pumpkin pie mix, eggs and vanilla together until smooth. Pour the mixture onto the crust and sprinkle it with the remaining topping mixture.

Bake the bars for 30 to 35 minutes, or until the topping is light golden brown. Cool in the pan before cutting into bars.

Cover and store leftover bars in an airtight container in the refrigerator for 4 to 5 days.

gooey pecan pie bars

These bars have the same irresistible pecan pie filling that's in a traditional pecan pie, but it's layered on top of a shortbread cookie crust rather than a piecrust. Did I mention how much easier they are to make than pie? Hello, new Thanksgiving dessert!

CRUST

2 cups (240 g) all-purpose flour

½ cup (100 g) granulated sugar

¼ tsp kosher salt

¾ cup (170 g) unsalted butter, cold

FILLING

1 cup (110 g) light brown sugar

1 cup (240 ml) light corn syrup

½ cup (115 g) unsalted butter

4 eggs, lightly beaten

2½ cups (275 g) finely chopped pecans

1 tsp vanilla extract

Preheat the oven to 350°F (180°C). Grease a 9 x 13–inch (22 x 33–cm) pan with butter or nonstick cooking spray and then line the pan with parchment paper, leaving an overhang on all sides. Grease the parchment with butter or nonstick cooking spray and then set it aside.

To make the crust, in a large mixing bowl, stir together the flour, sugar and salt. Using a pastry blender, cut in the butter until the mixture resembles fine crumbs. Press the mixture evenly into the prepared pan. Bake for 15 to 18 minutes, or until lightly browned; set it aside.

To make the filling, in a medium saucepan, combine the light brown sugar, corn syrup and butter. Bring to a boil over medium heat, stirring constantly. Remove it from the heat.

Place the eggs in a medium bowl. While continuously stirring, gradually add about ½ cup (120 ml) of the hot mixture into the eggs. Then add the mixture back to the saucepan. Stir in the pecans and vanilla until combined. Pour the nut mixture over the baked crust.

Bake for 30 to 32 minutes, or until the filling is set. Cool in the pan on a wire rack before cutting into bars.

Cover and store leftover bars in an airtight container in the refrigerator for 4 to 5 days.

no–bake bars

You know that time of year when the thought of turning the oven on leaves you hot under the collar (literally)? That's where these no-bake bars come in to save the day. And because there's no baking required to make these recipes, they are ridiculously easy to prepare and come together in nearly no time at all.

Take the No-Bake Peanut Butter Bars (page 128), for example. The recipe is a close cousin to Reese's peanut butter cups, except twenty times easier to make because there's no fooling around with mini cupcake pans or liners. They also contain a proper peanut butter to chocolate ratio, in my personal opinion. The Salted Brown Butter Rice Krispies Treats® (page 131) are a grown-up, gourmet version of the traditional treats that you never knew you needed until now. And the Cookie Butter Fudge (page 132)? Well, sweet treats don't get much easier or prettier than those.

Because each recipe in this chapter is so different, there are no overall tips and techniques for me to leave you with. Don't worry, though—I've included relevant tips for each recipe where applicable! Don't be surprised if the recipes in this chapter become your favorite. They already are for me!

no–bake peanut butter bars

If you have a peanut butter lover in your life, you have got to make them these. They're not overly sweet, and there's just the tiniest hint of crunch from the graham cracker crumbs. Also, the topping is smooth, creamy chocolate, blended with just a little bit more peanut butter. It's basically a Reese's on steroids, and they're begging for you to make them!

½ cup (115 g) unsalted butter, melted

1¼ cups (125 g) graham cracker crumbs, approximately 8 full-sheet graham crackers

1¾ cups (210 g) powdered sugar

1 cup + 3 tbsp (300 g) natural creamy peanut butter, divided

6 oz (170 g) 70% cacao dark chocolate, chopped

Line an 8 x 8–inch (20 x 20–cm) pan with aluminum foil or parchment paper and set it aside.

In a medium bowl, mix the melted butter, graham cracker crumbs and powdered sugar. Stir in 1 cup (250 g) of peanut butter, then press the mixture evenly into the prepared pan.

In a small bowl, melt the remaining 3 tablespoons (50 g) of peanut butter with the chopped chocolate in the microwave or on the stove in a double boiler. Stir until smooth. Spread evenly over the peanut butter layer.

Chill the bars in the refrigerator until completely firm, at least 2 hours. Allow them to sit at room temperature for 10 minutes before cutting. Serve chilled. (Setting them out for a few hours at room temperature for serving is OK.)

Cover leftover bars tightly and refrigerate for up to 1 week.

salted brown butter rice krispies treats®

Rice Krispies Treats®, whether purchased from the store or prepared according to the recipe on the cereal box, are pretty close to perfection, in my opinion. For years I saw no need to change them, but simplicity has its own way of inviting change, so I started tweaking the recipe, adding ingredients and changing some of the techniques to make a Rice Krispies Treat that's better than any I've ever eaten. That's the recipe I'm sharing here.

¾ cup (170 g) unsalted butter, cubed

½ tsp kosher salt

1½ tsp (8 ml) vanilla extract

10 oz (284 g) mini marshmallows

6 cups (170 g) Rice Krispies cereal

Line a 9 x 9–inch (22 x 22–cm) pan with aluminum foil or parchment paper, leaving an overhang on all sides. Set it aside.

Place the butter in a light-colored skillet. (The light-colored skillet will help you determine when the butter begins browning.) Melt the butter over medium heat, stirring constantly. Once melted, the butter will start to foam. Keep stirring. After 5 to 8 minutes, the butter will begin browning; you'll notice lightly browned specks begin to form at the bottom of the pan, and you'll start to smell a nutty aroma. Once browned, immediately remove from the heat, then stir in the salt and vanilla.

Working quickly, add half of the marshmallows and stir until thoroughly melted. Add the remaining marshmallows and stir until melted. (The residual heat from the butter should be enough to melt them without adding the heat, but you can return the pot to medium-low heat for a few minutes if the second addition of marshmallows isn't melting quickly.)

Add the cereal and gently fold it in with a rubber spatula coated in nonstick cooking spray until the cereal is completely covered with the marshmallow mixture.

Transfer the mixture to the prepared pan. Using the rubber spatula, gently press the mixture into an even layer.

Let the treats stand at room temperature until set, about 1 hour, before cutting into bars.

The treats can be stored in an airtight container at room temperature for up to 5 days.

NOTES: *After you add the marshmallows, keep the heat on low or below medium-low. If your marshmallow is exposed to heat that's too high, you'll end up with treats hard enough to break your teeth!*

Don't pack the Rice Krispies Treats into the pan too tightly; gently spread them evenly into your prepared pan. If you pack them in too tightly, then they could end up too dense and be difficult to bite through.

cookie butter fudge

This quick fudge recipe is very forgiving and lends itself well to customization. And since it takes only five minutes to whip up a batch, you can make multiple variations in a really short amount of time. You could swirl in some crushed gingersnap cookies into the fudge before you pop it into the fridge to help intensify the flavor and add a little crunch, or switch up the white chocolate chips with peanut butter or butterscotch chips to create different flavor combinations. Go wild!

1¼ cups (225 g) white chocolate chips

14 oz (420 ml) sweetened condensed milk, divided

½ tsp kosher salt, divided

1¼ cups (220 g) semisweet chocolate chips

½ cup (130 g) cookie butter, divided

Prepare an 8 x 8–inch (20 x 20–cm) pan by lining it with aluminum foil and spraying the foil lightly with nonstick cooking spray.

In a medium microwave-safe bowl, combine the white chocolate chips, 7 ounces (210 ml) of sweetened condensed milk and ¼ teaspoon of salt. In a separate medium microwave-safe bowl, place the semisweet chocolate chips, the remaining 7 ounces (210 ml) of sweetened condensed milk and the remaining ¼ teaspoon of salt.

Microwave the white chocolate mixture, stirring after every 30 seconds, until it's melted and smooth. Repeat this same procedure with the bowl of semisweet chocolate chips, until both mixtures are smooth. Stir in ¼ cup (65 g) of cookie butter into each mixture until smooth and combined.

Using a large spoon, place alternate dollops of the white and dark chocolate mixtures in the prepared pan. This doesn't have to be neat or precise; you just want to make sure that the chocolates are well mixed and one is not primarily on top or bottom.

Take a toothpick and swirl it through the pan, mixing the two chocolates until they're in a pretty marbled pattern. Don't swirl too much or your swirls will become muddy and indistinct.

Cover the pan with plastic wrap and place it in the refrigerator to chill until fully set, 1 to 2 hours. Once the fudge is set, remove it from the pan and cut it into small squares.

For the best taste and texture, serve this fudge at room temperature.

Store the fudge in an airtight container in the refrigerator for up to 2 weeks.

payday® bars

*These simple bars have a peanut butter caramel-like core with salted peanuts
in every bite. Personally, I like them plain, but I also like to take things a step further
and give them a good dunking in some melted semisweet chocolate!
Try them both ways and see which you like best!*

16 oz (450 g) salted cocktail peanuts, divided

¼ cup (58 g) unsalted butter

10 oz (284 g) peanut butter chips

14 oz (420 ml) sweetened condensed milk

2 cups (100 g) miniature marshmallows

Prepare a 9 x 13–inch (22 x 33–cm) pan by lining it with aluminum foil and lightly spraying the foil with nonstick cooking spray. Pour half of the peanuts on the bottom of the pan.

In a saucepan over medium heat, combine the butter and peanut butter chips. Stir occasionally until fully melted. Remove the pan from the heat and add the sweetened condensed milk and then the marshmallows (do not melt the marshmallows).

Pour the mixture over the peanuts in the prepared pan and spread evenly. Pour the remaining peanuts on top and pat down lightly. Place the bars in the fridge and chill for 1 hour before slicing.

Cover and store leftover bars in an airtight container at room temperature for 7 days.

acknowledgments

Writing this cookbook has been a stressful yet wonderful, collaborative experience from start to finish. If this book brings you happiness and a full stomach, it's in large part because of the huge support network of family, friends and fellow bakers that helped me. I'm thrilled to have this opportunity to thank all those who've contributed everything from recipes to photography props to sage advice at crucial moments.

To Madeline Greenhalgh, Meg Baskis and the entire team at Page Street Publishing Co., this book wouldn't have been possible without your enthusiasm, support and hard work.

To my incredible recipe testers: Anna Price, Jenna Barnard, Dee Frances, Nick Yarbrough, Julia Estrada, Jennifer Switzer, Allison Clayton and Samantha Jones, thank you for baking your way through all 50 recipes to make sure they were ready to share.

To my fellow bakers and food bloggers who helped troubleshoot my baking issues, contributed base recipes for me to work from and listened to my endless venting, raging and ranting: Ari Laing, Cosette Posko, Erin Clarkson, Jase Kingsland-Shim, Sarah Fennel, Jennifer Switzer, LeAnne Shor, Jenna Barnard, Michelle Lopez, Sam Adler, Michele Song, Jamie Silva and so many more. Thank you for your words of encouragement throughout the entire cookbook journey and for always helping keep me sane.

To all my past coworkers who support Mike Bakes NYC, especially Will Tock, Megan West, Alessandra Ambrosi, Tammy Vadasz, Najah Zeidan, Benjamin Silver, Devin Horzempa, Ryan McCabe, Stephen Fields, Jonathan Boyce, Josiel Calcano, Michael Rosen, Ms. Joyce and Ms. Janet. Thank you for always making weekdays more bearable, for taste-testing everything and always giving honest feedback (even when you knew I wouldn't like it).

To my forever friends: Stephen Wah, Taylor Brown, Alodie Efamba, Samantha Hamidan, Esther Kim and Janae Hunte. You guys have been there since the beginning of Mike Bakes NYC. Thank you for always providing much-needed distractions, inspiration, support and laughter.

To my grandparents, Richard and Marsha Bramhall, who have been my biggest cheerleaders along the way. And to my mom, Angela Johnson, for teaching me to be a hard worker and for always loving, supporting and encouraging me.

And finally, to all the readers of Mike Bakes NYC. THANK YOU FOR EVERYTHING. I mean it. None of this would have happened without you guys.

about the author

Mike Johnson is the baker, blogger and photographer behind Mike Bakes NYC, a popular baking blog and Instagram account. His work has appeared on- and offline in *Bake from Scratch* magazine, *Bake from Scratch: Volume Four*, BuzzFeed, feedfeed and Food52. While baking and blogging, Mike also works full-time as an attorney. He currently lives in New York City. *Even Better Brownies* is his first book.

index